DAPPLE

A LAND G...

DAPPLED SUNLIGHT
A LAND GIRL'S STORY

Elise Johns

ARTHUR H. STOCKWELL LTD.
Elms Court   Ilfracombe   Devon
Established 1898

British Library Cataloguing-in-Publication Data.
A catalogue record for this book is available
from the British Library.

For
David, Caroline
and Adrianna

ISBN 0 7223 3203-3
Printed in Great Britain by
Arthur H. Stockwell Ltd.
Elms Court   Ilfracombe
Devon

CONTENTS

A Land Girls' Rally at Newton St. Cyres, 1944.

An organized visit to the Theatre Royal, Exeter, 1945,
when we wore our new berets.

INTRODUCTION

Have you ever walked through a tree-lined avenue on a summer day, and watched the kaleidoscope of colours and patterns created by the sun's rays, piercing through the green canopy above? The dancing shafts of light replacing shadows, brightness replacing gloom, portray for me a symbol of the ups and downs of life, the good times and the not-so-good. Most people experience these highs and lows as the years roll by — few escape. But for my part, as I recall my years as a land girl, the image of the dancing shadows seems a particularly apt way to describe how I felt during the years 1943–49. The sun was always there, high above, but occasionally, so too, were the shadows, although as I look back through the rose-tinted spectacles of nostalgia, the gloom was short-lived, and life was good.

But before I launch into the story of my life as a land girl, it seems only logical that I should give a brief outline of my early years, and how it all came about.

I was the youngest of three children, my brother, the eldest, was seven years my senior, and my sister was nearly five years old when I was born. We were, what today would be termed as a one-parent family, our father died when I was just two. Looking back, I feel that we had a happy and well balanced childhood, although I suspect I probably had the best of it, as the baby of the family. Toys were few, but what we could do with a few empty cardboard boxes was amazing. However, books were not in short supply, and my earliest memories are of being read to, at first the usual children's books, but by the age of around six, my sister read books to me well beyond my age range, and explained it all as we went along, this instilled in me a love of literature and reading that is with me to this day. I cannot say I missed having a father, probably because my brother filled the gap.

My sister must have been very patient with me, a five year space is a lot when young, and we were good friends. Together we went for long walks, as children could in those days, without fear. We collected wild flowers, peeped into birds' nests and picked wild strawberries and blackberries, and nuts as the seasons changed.

Just before Christmas, we went to a wood where we gathered holly sprays loaded with berries and small fir branches that became our Christmas tree decorated with cut-out bells and stars that my sister made from cardboard, covered with shiny paper. My mother produced the angel that was tied to the top — it must have been around for years, as it was pretty tatty really, but to me it spelled magic. Yes, we did quarrel occasionally, and I suspect now, that being so much younger, I was usually the source of the friction, and that most times it was me who got my own way. But, as children do, we grew up with the passing years. I spent five of the happiest years of my life in the local grammar school, enjoying the responsibility, the challenges of both class room and sports field, and my heart was heavy indeed when I left, after taking my School Leaving Exam, as it was called in those days. I had done very well. No, I am not boasting, but adding weight to my mother's wish that I should do something with my life. From an early age, we were all aware that we would one day have to earn our own living, but this had been put on the back burner during my school-days. Now it had become a reality, and a problem that had to be tackled very soon.

So it was that, partly to please my mother, and also to get started in employment, I applied for a job at a local bank. I was given an interview, and offered the post, and told to start the following week. I can still remember what misery I endured, whilst I contemplated what life would be like, cooped up in an office for eight or nine hours a day, and was torn between my desire to please my mother, and the absolute certainty that such a life would strangle me. The war had come, like an evil, black cloud, and all young people would be called to war work unless in a reserved occupation. Meanwhile, my sister had joined the Women's Land Army and was working in deepest Cornwall. From her letters, I could tell it was not a bed of roses, picking frosted sprouts, cutting cauliflowers, and scrubbing off swede turnips with cold water, but the more I thought about it, the more convinced I became, that, at least for the duration of the war, this was the life for me. I must say that my Mother took it pretty well; with a mother's intuition, she probably realized how unhappy I was with the prospect of the bank job, although I thought I'd done a good job at hiding it from her.

And so it was that in April 1943, at the tender age of seventeen years, I left home to do my bit for the war effort, and earn my living at the same time. How callous the young can be! It didn't occur to me that my mother was probably very sad to see her youngest child set off for an unknown destination, but all I felt was a sense of excitement at the prospect of a challenge to come.

CHAPTER ONE

A NEW LIFE

It was a glorious day when I stepped off the train at Bideford station, and looked anxiously round for my first employer. A middle-aged man approached me, accompanied by a slim young woman, about 23 years of age, who was introduced to me as Eleanor. Mr Norris picked up my small suitcase and together we made our way outside, to a large car with a trailer hitched up behind. The trailer was filled with milk churns and every available bit of space inside the car was filled with milk bottles. However, a shuffle around of the bottle crates, and I was able to squeeze inside and my case piled onto the bottles. My feelings were an odd mixture of excitement and trepidation, as, in my new uniform we headed towards Higher Alminstone, my future place of work. The country looked so lovely, with the occasional glimpse of the sea, that I cheered up and told myself that at least this was a beautiful place to be.

The next day I began in earnest, and flung myself into my new life with enthusiasm and a desire to please and prove my worth. My main job was to help the other girl in the dairy. The milk from the Tuberculin Tested cows on the farm did not go off to the factory over at Torrington, but was sold over quite a large area, either in churns or bottles. Various dairies in Bideford and Barnstaple, hospitals and schools were the customers, and the milk had to be measured carefully into the churns, or bottled up, and then the churns and the bottles had to be loaded onto the trailer, and into the car, for the young roundsman to deliver.

My employer had one of the largest herds in the district at that time, and even so, quite often more milk had to be bought in from local farms, whose cows were TB attested, but more about that later. The churns were the old heavy type with twelve gallon capacity, nicknamed 'Long Toms', and the first job of the day was to get these brutes on to the trailer.

There was a knack in swinging these on board, and also knowing just when to let go of the handle. After several mishaps, resulting in crushed and bleeding fingers, I got the hang of it and also learnt how to roll the full churns along on their lower rim to avoid carrying them further than necessary.

1

Of course it was very important that the bottles and churns were kept scrupulously clean. A large boiler heated water for the bottle washing and also produced steam for sterilizing the churns. The sterilizer consisted of a small platform with holes, over which the inverted churn was placed, and then the steam was turned on, and hey presto! a churn ready to receive a fresh supply of milk. Of course the churns first had to be scrubbed off both inside and out, by hand, using a churn brush and water with a potent cleaning agent added to it. This came in a metal container — plastic was still unknown — and a metal scoop was provided to put the jelly-like substance into the hot water. The cleaning agent was, I think, caustic acid, and soon the flimsy handle on the scoop was literally eaten away; so we scooped without the handle, and fingers and nails bore witness. It was called 'Lavaloid' I remember, and I expect it was efficient, but not to be recommended for improving the appearance of one's hands!

What a godsend that boiler was! We ate our mid-day snack huddled beside it, and during the winter months we dried our sodden clothes on it. A real source of comfort.

My work in the dairy usually took all morning and in the afternoons I was able to do other farm jobs, which I preferred. Besides the dairy girl, there was Eleanor, whom I have already mentioned, and another girl called Doris who did the retail milk round at Bucks Mills. These two girls lived in the farmhouse and did the milking. The cows were milked in a long shed, where 20 animals could be tied up, and there was a milking machine which was not very common then. The front of the milking shed was open, so there were times when it was far from comfortable for the girls. As there were more than twenty cows to be milked, when four of five were milked, they would be let out, and their places taken by unmilked animals. This was the procedure until all had been through the shed. Also working on the farm was the young man who did the milk round and turned his hand to other jobs when he got back from his rounds. In addition were two men who were occupied with cleaning out the shippons, calf sheds and, of course, the field work. Today, that sounds a bit staff, but one has to remember there was no tractor, and so all jobs had to be done either by horse power or by hand.

At first, as I joined the men at work, I was on the receiving end of much leg-pulling and practical jokes and heard words I had never heard before, and expressions that were totally new to me. I was a

2

pretty naïve seventeen-year-old and had had a fairly strict Victorian upbringing, so it all came as a bit of a shock. But there was a war on, and I felt that everyone had to suffer and pay a price of some kind, and if my small sacrifice was to have to endure the ribald jokes — well, so be it! I much preferred the field work, it was far more varied and interesting than bottle filling and churn scrubbing. Sometimes, during particularly busy spells, I would be out all day, and the dairy girl would have to manage without me, albeit with some moans and groans. On this farm, no cereals were grown but large quantities of flat pole cabbages and mangolds. The spindly cabbage plants arrived on farm in May, tied up in bundles of 200 and there was a frantic rush to get them dug in before they wilted too much.

Equipped with diggers we proceeded either to drop the plants down through a drill then to go back to the end and dig them in, or someone would hand the plants to each digger as they moved along. It was back-breaking work, but the secret was to stay bent over, and not to straighten up for anything. We tucked a few extra plants in our belts — a piece of binder twine tied around the waist — in case we found a gap with no plant waiting, or came across a broken plant.

There was an element of skill in handing the plants; they had to be presented to the digger root first and a fumbled or missed pass earned a swift oath. As for the digger, as one moved forward to dig another plant into the ridged up soil one contrived to tread in the previous plant, ensuring it was well secure. There was a steady rhythm in the job that appealed to me, you might think it very monotonous and back breaking, but, after a couple of days the backache eased, and I got a glow of satisfaction at seeing the job completed. But alas! that was only the beginning! a few weeks later we were back in the same fields, but this time armed with a turnip hoe, to tackle the weeds that had appeared from nowhere, and were threatening to choke the young plants. I ran into a snag straight away. I use any tool with a handle 'right hand afore' and all the men used theirs 'left hand in front'. So I had to hoe apart from them, to avoid a double lot of weed being pulled into one space between the rows. I soon got the hang of it, and tried hard to keep up with the men, and eventually did. I have known occasions when the weed was allowed to grow too far and it had to be pulled by hand, not a desirable job, as often there were nettles and thistles lurking amongst the other weeds and still we couldn't close the gates on the cabbages.

To keep the ground clean and weed free between the rows of plants, a horse drawn hoe called a skerifier was used. The horse had to be led and you have guessed it! this was my job, holding onto the horse's head, up and down, down and up, for hours and days on end, the flies biting us and the horse, the dust rising, and blisters punishing our feet. Once the cabbage plants really began to grow, they smothered the weed but the reverse would have been the case without the hoeing.

Now the mangold crop was a bit different, they were planted by horse-drawn seed drill so we were spared the digging chore. However, they too needed hoeing, not once, but twice. The first time we side hoed them, pulling the weeds away from the drills of little plants, then, a couple of weeks later, when the plants had grown quite a bit, we singled them out, an operation by which most of the plants were pulled out leaving the remaining plants with a space to grow. I noticed that the boss, and the two girls who lived in, spent only brief periods in the fields and they kept apart from the rest of us. They were never there long enough to get aching backs. Of course they had the milking to do, so I suppose their time was limited. Once again, the horse drawn skerifier had to be used, and I scarcely needed telling what my job was to be!

Once these crops had been cared for, I was still kept pretty busy. Quite a lot of poultry was kept in field arks, these consisted of a covered roosting and laying area one end and a netting covered run the other. Every day these arks had to be moved along on to fresh territory, some had to be levered along using a stout pole, others had a handle sticking out that one grasped, and man-handled it along. They were heavy things, especially when waterlogged and when the ground was sodden and muddy, no easy task as there were about a dozen of them. But now it was time to give them their annual coat of creosote, both inside and out. Doing the outside was a piece of cake, but crawling around in the confined space inside, was no joke. I'm afraid quite a lot of creosote got spilt, not only on the ground but my arms and face got liberally splashed, and because my skin was still pretty delicate, I suffered a lot, as areas of my arms and face became inflamed and painful.

But in the meantime, my personal life brightened up considerably. I had not been very happy in my digs, but then I had the chance to move, and Emily was a dear. She took me under her wing, made me feel so welcome and treated me like a daughter.

4

Also, I now had a boy friend, the same young man who drove and did the milk delivery rounds. I suppose in some ways, it wasn't the best situation to be working alongside one's boy friend, but we kept work and pleasure strictly divided and after the usual banter from the men, everything went on as before.

CHAPTER TWO

HARVESTING THE GRASS

Now that the root crops had been tended to, it was time to harvest the grass that had grown lush and tall, to provide winter fodder for the cattle. On this farm, it was all made into silage which was not common practice in those days, most farmers preferring to make hay. Nobody knew anything about cutting the grass before it came into flower, and nobody had heard about dry matter or sugar content, so, by today's high standards, it must have been pretty poor quality. It was cut by a horse drawn mowing machine and hard work it was for the horse. A long blade with a deeply serrated edge shuttled to and fro at high speed, cutting through the grass, and a piece of timber called a swathe board on the outer end of the blade ensured that the grass was left in rows on the ground.

The knives got blunted very quickly, so there were replacement knives at the ready, and one man sat at the corner of the field sharpening the knives with a file. Quite often, the blades would catch on a stone so there had to be replacements for these too, the broken one knocked out and a new one riveted onto the blades. After a few rounds had been cut, our work began. We used a fork to make two rows into one. The grass was heavy and full of sap so it was quite hard, beside being a lengthy task. But worse was to follow, when the horses and wagons appeared we had to hoist the grass up on to the carts, where a man levelled it about to 'make the load'. Again, no one had been told about the advantages of wilting the grass, and as we shoved the wet and heavy crop up onto the trailers, bits fell back on us, and some found it's way inside our shirts.

The boss had wooden silos, made in sections that were bolted together to form a large ring, about six feet high. I never saw their like anywhere else. The grass was off-loaded into this wooden ring, and when this was filled, another ring was bolted onto the first one, thereby increasing the height, so the job of pitching up the grass got progressively harder. Inside the silo, two men put the grass about to keep it level. Now the boss had read some enlightening article that suggested that the addition of molasses added to the palatability and feed value of the silage, and also that any efforts made to compress the ensiled grass were also beneficial. So after every fresh load put into the silo, molasses was applied, using a watering can and every morning, before the loads started coming in again, Eleanor and I climbed into the pit to tread it down.

Neither of us was very heavy, so I doubt that we did much good, but we marched round and round and occasionally added a few standing jumps for good measure. The legs of our dungarees became sticky and dark brown with the molasses, but it was some relief to see that the pile had sunk a little overnight which would give a bit of a respite for the unloading of the first wagonfull. But it soon piled up again, and when a third ring was fixed up my heart sank, and I could not see how we were going to get the grass up to that height. However, one small section was left out, providing a sort of hatchway through which we pitched in the grass.

There were two of these silos, and when they were both filled, the rest of the grass was just piled into a large heap, and of course, none of it was covered, so the waste was pretty bad. When I see today's sophisticated machinery, and watch trailers being loaded mechanically, and changed over without so much as the need to get off the tractor seat, it makes me aware of the staggering developments there have been over the last fifty years or so. Only one cut was taken off a field then, unlike now, when two, three or even four per season is common practice. Mind you, fertilizer was not chucked around as it is today, partly because it was difficult to come by during the war years.

For a few weeks we were occupied, doing odd jobs around the farm. The men put tiles on roofs, hung new gates and such-like. The wagons needed some repairs after the bashing they had taken during the harvest. I was given a hook, and used it to slash off thistles and nettles around the buildings, getting stung in the process. Emily skilfully removed the prickles lodged in my fingers, with a needle which she first jabbed into carbolic soap.

One day I was given a heavy tool, a double headed job on a wooden stick, and told to go to a certain field where the docks, and

6

large thistles we called "row-dashels" were flourishing. It was necessary to get all the roots out, as any left behind would produce a healthy plant next year. On one occasion I got the spiked end well under the roots of a particularly big dock, and attempted to lever it out by pulling hard back on the handle. I heard a cracking noise and was dismayed to see the handle had split. So, I had to return to the farm and show the boss the broken implement. He was not overly pleased. I expect the handle was already weak, and I had merely finished it off, but he didn't take kindly to what he considered was carelessness.

CHAPTER THREE

THE WINTER

As the days now began to get shorter and the sun less powerful, we prepared for winter, but first the potato crop had to be harvested. A mechanical potato digger was available on loan, from the Ministry of Agriculture and it was a case of waiting one's turn. The drill was that you had to collect it from the farm where it was last used, and the next on the list fetched it from you, a reasonably fair procedure.

During the war, every farmer had, by law, to grow potatoes as it constituted a staple item for the national food supply, and was also fed to livestock. Many farmers, my boss included, hired gangs to expedite the harvesting. These gangs were usually land girls, like myself, but they fell into another category altogether. They lived in hostels and usually worked as groups on different farms, so they knew little or nothing about some jobs, i.e., calf rearing, milking or dairy work, but became jolly skilled at such jobs as hoeing and harvesting.

Beside these gangs, we got help from neighbouring farmers, on the basis that we sent back to help them when they got the digger, a sort of lease-lend affair. The length of the potato row was carefully paced out and divided up between the number of hands employed, and marked out with sticks stuck in the ground. Depending on the staff available, we picked alone or in pairs. We were given a large wooden basket called a mawn, and also a bucket for small damaged tubers classed as 'pig' potatoes. The machine turned the potatoes out onto the ground, and wisely we stood clear as this was being done as often stones came flying out as well! We had some capers with these girls I well remember. They would slyly move the sticks if they thought they could get away with it, to reduce their stint, and when spotted, fierce arguments broke out, they would swear like navvies, but I never actually saw blows exchanged.

The potatoes were tipped into hessian sacks and every effort was made to get these under cover before we left work as an overnight shower could make a right old mess of the sacks. Some were stored in houses but when there was no more room, they were tipped onto the ground in a long heap, called a clamp, which had to be covered up. It was a skilful job, using clods of earth and straw, this was necessary to protect the tubers from rain and frost during the winter.

The importance of this job was illustrated the following spring when the clamp was opened up and it was an unhappy situation if a large quantity of potatoes was found to have been frosted and spoiled. Sometimes the weather was grand, golden autumn days when it seemed that summer refused to leave. At other times, it could be bitterly cold and to protect our backs from a spiteful wind, we tied sacks around our waists — a great help.

The mangolds were next on the list, but no digger for this crop, just our hands. Armed with a wickedly sharp knife, we moved along the drills tugging the roots out of the ground, and slashing the tops off with the knife, throwing two rows together as we did so. Once again, I had to learn by harsh experience, as I set about cutting off the leaves with more enthusiasm than skill, and after the knife had slipped on a rotten leaf, badly cutting my fingers, I was shown how to do it with a greater degree of safety.

The secret was to pull with the left hand and let the leaf stems fall across the upturned blade, the weight of the root did the rest, and fingers escaped intact. The defoliated roots then had to be loaded onto a horse drawn cart and taken to a dry corner where a huge heap was made of them, another clamp in fact where they too were protected by straw. This was not as meticulously done as in the case of potatoes, firstly because they would soon be needed to feed the cows and secondly because if a mangold took frost, it did not spoil the root and the frost would come out of it when the temperature rose.

To load the mangolds, we worked either side of the cart and flung them up by hand, and, as the load became higher, some of the roots would roll out over the side, either by accident, or sometimes, I confess, by mischievous intent and land with a thud on the bent back of the worker on the other side. This usually resulted in an oath and a muttered threat, and so the same thing would happen to you, just when you thought all was forgiven and forgotten!

By now, winter was really upon us and I exchanged the cotton shirt and dungarees for corduroy breeches and a thick pullover. Nobody had waterproof protective clothing, so the best we could do was to drape a hessian sack around our shoulders, secured with a nail, and another sack about our waist, tied round with binder cord, rather like an ungainly apron. There was a severe shortage of rubber, because it was needed for service lorry tyres, aeroplane tyres and many other vital things. So, we had no Wellington boots but had been kitted out with two pairs of leather boots and canvas leggings. I believe these boots were of good quality but they got waterlogged after hours spent ankle deep in mud, so one's feet were usually damp and cold, and in the early days my feet suffered badly. One pair of boots rubbed my toes, the other pair was harsher on my heels, so I worked out a sort of rota system whereby I wore pair 'A' till my heels were raw and then switched to pair 'B' to allow my heels to recover, but punishing my poor toes instead. But after about eighteen months, my skin had hardened and I was able to walk around without the agony I had first endured.

But to get back to winter and its activities. I was now introduced to the two farm horses — oh yes — I'd been aware of them from day one and had led them in the root fields — but this was different. I was shown how to harness them up and how to tackle them into the cart or butt. Now a butt was a smaller version of a cart and with one distinct advantage — it could be tipped up, allowing its load to slide off onto the ground. The tail board at the back was first removed then a long iron rod, called a trip-stick, was removed from the front end and by moving the horse forward a couple of paces, the actual body of the cart tipped up and the job was done!

I should add that there was a skill in loading a butt properly, evenly, in fact. Too much at the front end or foreloaded resulted in too much weight on the horse's back, too much weight at the rear end, or back loaded and it made the load uncomfortable for the horse to pull. The two horses were named Tidy and Punch. Now Punch was a big powerful animal, but he had one wicked characteristic, he would bite! For some reason, he hated being backed, i.e., moving in reverse gear, neither did he approve of anyone reaching under his belly and of course, this was necessary to secure the big strap, known as a belly-band, that kept all the harness in place. I still carry a scar on my thumb where he displayed his malice by grinding his teeth on my hand, and had numerous bites on my arms, but as they were usually protected by my sleeves, no evidence of those remain. Tidy was a smart and good tempered mare, she behaved beautifully and was very tender mouthed, which meant she responded well to any pull on the reins. But she was headstrong, and too fast to be suitable for the skerifier, but ideal for shaft work.

One day I was standing in the empty butt, pulled by Tidy, as we headed for home. She probably sensed it was the end of the day and boy! was she in a hurry! We had to negotiate a sharp bend before reaching the stables and she was in overdrive. I expect my lack of driving experience was at fault, because one wheel of the butt went over the wheelbarrow that had been parked upside down, and over a muck heap. The weight of the butt albeit empty, crushed it flat, almost beyond repair. I say almost because it must have been a favourite with my boss, and so after sternly ticking me off, he set about repairing it, and to my dismay, made a jolly good job of it. Dismay? yes, it was the most unwieldy, heavy barrow I've ever seen, before or since, it must have weighed fifty six pounds or more when empty, especially if waterlogged. Made all of wood, the handles were hefty extensions of the sides and rough, causing galls on my hands. How I loathed that barrow.

I know that my dislike was shared by another member of the staff at least. For a time, a man came to work who was both deaf and dumb. However, he could write; apparently he had been to a special school which is amazing for those days. He was mentally quite alert and from time to time, notes were exchanged between him and other members of the staff, also the boss. Well, he took one look at that wheelbarrow and gave it the thumbs down, so to speak. He informed the boss — by a note — that he intended to bring along his own model. And so he did. It was certainly a lighter, more manoeuvrable barrow, but the added gadget was what amazed everyone. It had brakes, operated by a wire and lever below one handle, similar to the calliper brakes on bicycles. He displayed it to us with much noise and arm waving but I'm sorry to say the chaps

10

were not greatly impressed. In fact, one bloke was heard to mutter darkly, "I've always found I had to push the b----- thing, can't see the need of brakes."

CHAPTER FOUR

THE LOCAL SMITHY

Of course the two horses required new shoes from time to time and one Friday afternoon, at leave work time, my boss told me to be at the farm at 7 a.m. the next day to make a trip to Parkham where the nearest blacksmiths plied their trade. It was pitch dark at that hour but the boss was up and he set me on my way. Tidy had fallen very lame, so Punch was kitted out with halter, neck collar and hames, and Tidy's halter was tied to Punch's hames to help drag her along. A dry sack was thrown over Punch's back and I was given a leg up. Poor old Tidy hung back and was literally dragged along, and Punch wasn't very happy about it either, I could tell that by the nasty look in his eye when his head jerked around.

Progress was slow and I decided that it would be better if I rode the mare instead, and encouraged her along with an occasional dig in the ribs with the heels of my boots. There is an old saying about changing horses in mid stream, well, I wasn't in the middle of a stream, but in the middle of nowhere, and it was still quite dark. As I prepared to move on to Tidy's back, she shied away and I slid clumsily to the ground between the two horses. How to get on board again was the burning question, they were big animals, and there was no way I could leap onto either back, without a leg up. I managed to manoeuvre Punch near a hedge, and with a leap and a prayer, I was aloft again, but alas! the sack had disappeared in the gloom. Better the devil you know! I did not attempt to transfer again, and had only myself to blame for having lost the thin cushion under my bottom.

Dawn had broken when I reached the smithy and from a bungalow alongside, the blacksmith emerged with a string of oaths, and demanded to know what I was doing there at that ungodly hour. Timidly I explained whose horses they were and that they both needed new shoes. He grunted and returned inside, presumably to finish his breakfast. Then his lady wife came out, what a contrast, she was a large woman with a pleasant smile. I think she took pity on the skinny desolate girl who stood there, because she beckoned me inside, bade me sit at the table and set a large plate of fried breakfast in front of me. There were several thick slices of home cured bacon, well fried and with a delicious salty, crunchy texture sitting on a huge dollop of greasy, fried potato on which nestled — joy-of-joys, a lovely fried egg, sunny side up! What a feast that was, no dog could have left its plate cleaner. By now, the smith too, had mellowed and began to question me as to what time I had left the farm, where I came from, and how old I was. A couple of cups of strong tea and he was ready to start. Of course I had never seen this done before so I watched his every move, and marvelled at the way this wiry little man was able to hold those huge feet between his knees whilst he pared their hooves and fitted the new shoes. He cursed the horses too, if they showed any signs of misbehaving, but I got the distinct impression he really loved them.

As it was a Saturday, only two or three other farmers arrived with their horses, and I expect I was something of a curiosity to them. At last it was done and the smith found another sack for me to sit on — I did not disclose how I had lost the other one — and helped me up onto Punch's back. He bade me a cheery farewell and I was on my way. What a relief it must have been for Tidy, it was she who took the lead and we got back in record time.

The men had told me it was recognized as being half a day's work to take a pair of horses for shoeing, so I was confident I could put the horses in the stable, give them some hay, and head for home. But not a bit of it. My boss had left orders that I was to take Punch and the cart to a farm about 2 miles away and bring back a load of silage.

I should explain that the boss bought fields of grass from other farmers, cut it and made extra silage. Sometimes it would be brought back to the farm at the time of the harvest, and sometimes a silo would be set up at the other farm and the silage brought back during the winter months as and when required. So Punch had to be tackled in to the trailer with the customary game of avoiding his snapping jaws. The trailer was large, it was the product of a workshop situated in Torridge Hill, Bideford and owned by a family called Violet. To own a Violet trailer was much desired, it had tyres and bowled along quite nicely.

When I reached the silo, I could see that stock had been milling around it and this had turned the ground into a quagmire over a considerable area. My lack of experience was my undoing. I positioned the trailer close to the silo and proceeded to load it up. At last, I calculated I had got a good load so I jumped down from the silo, waded through the mud and gave Punch an encouraging tug on the bridle. He gave one almighty heave but nothing happened. Even making allowances for the mud, he was a strong horse and willing with it, but repeated attempts to move were of no avail. I decided to seek help from the farmer and trudged across a couple of fields and knocked on the farmhouse door. I didn't think he looked too pleased and reflected that he, too was probably in the middle of a meal.

When we got back to the silo, he soon solved the problem. The wheels had quite large hubs and the weight of the load had made the wheel sink against the silo, just where two sections were bolted together. No way could the hub pass the joint and no way could Punch reverse the trailer in that morass. It would have taken an elephant to tug it out, probably demolishing the silo in the process. "Only one thing for it," said he, "it will have to be offloaded." Away he went, no doubt to finish his interrupted meal.

To be fair, his behaviour was very much the exception, nearly all country people I met were helpful and encouraging, especially, I suspect, as word was getting around that I was not afraid of work. Now it was out of the question that I throw the silage onto the ground, with all that mud around, so I had no option but to heave it back up onto the silo. Finally, I was able to move the horse and trailer and position it so that there would not be a problem. So much for my half day! It was mid afternoon by the time I had unloaded the silage back at the farm, unharnessed the horse and returned him to the stable. The wonderful breakfast I had eaten so many hours before was just a fond memory. I was very muddy, tired and hungry.

Emily was most concerned, bless her! and placed my dried out plate of dinner in front of me, accompanied by suitable noises of sympathy as I unfolded my sorry tale between mouthfuls of food. Dried up it might have been, but I devoured it ravenously and gradually my ill-humour drifted away. I should point out that we never got paid a penny extra for overtime, but a promise of some time off later, and one had to practically kneel before the boss to claim this.

On the other hand, there was an occasion when my brother came to see me. No doubt my mother was anxious about my well being;

she made it clear she was not happy with what I was doing and of course I could see her point. A daughter who had left school with passes in nine subjects of the School Certificate, five with distinction, was surely wasting her education and abilities, working in fields and cow-sheds, and I'm glad to say she didn't know the half of it!

Anyway, when my brother arrived, I proudly showed him the milking machine, still an object to marvel at in those days, the cows, and calves, and other things of interest. They knew he was there right enough, but no one offered him a cup of tea and he had cycled eighteen miles on an old bicycle with no gears, and when pay day came round, I had one shilling docked for time lost whilst he was there!

CHAPTER FIVE

CARTING

By late November winter had really taken over, it seemed always to be raining or blowing a gale, often both. The cows were now kept in at night, and the muck heap grew at an amazing rate, as the shippens were cleaned out every day. When the heap resembled a mini version of the Great Pyramid at Giza, it was time to do something about it. The muck was loaded onto the butt and then taken to the fields where it was put in tidy rows of heaps, to be spread later by hand. That first winter it seemed to me that I was either carting the stuff, or spreading it come rain, frost or snow.

I was on the job week in, week out, often wet to the skin or very cold, probably both. What began to annoy me was the fact that, although the men helped load up, they then had inside jobs, whereas I, a girl, was out all day. Emily used to say, "You'll suffer for this one day my girl." Thank God I never have, but I confess I began to get a bit disgruntled and reckoned I was getting the dirty end of the stick.

Spreading the muck was a job that I hated, not because I was squeamish, far from it, but the continued throwing around of the heavy manure used to make the muscles around my stomach very sore, and also I used to get nauseous and often only picked at my dinner. Some few years after, I do recall spreading some muck for a local farmer in the evening, to earn a few bob, by that time I had got used to the job I guess.

Sometimes I would be sent out to the field, to cut and bring in a load of cabbages. We cut the cabbages with a hook and loaded them with a fork; most times they were wet and always heavy, but it was a change.

Another job came my way from time-to-time, and that was to get a load of mangolds from the clamp, and throw them out in a grass field, for the cows to eat the next day. One set the horse going across the field and hoped he would keep going whilst one tossed the roots out with a fork. Every so often, one would realize that the horse — crafty blighter! — was heading back to the gate, so a quick scramble to the front and a jerk of the reins was needed to get him back on course, often the roots formed figures of eight on the field, but it didn't really matter, the cows would find them.

A neighbouring small farmer had a right-of-way across one of these fields to reach a couple of little fields he owned. So many cows and the constant use of this track by horse and cart had rendered it into a fair resemblance of the Sargasso Sea, literally knee-deep in mud. The poor man complained to my boss about it, to which the boss replied — "Yes, it's a strange sort of concrete, it just never sets." So much for neighbourly goodwill.

CHAPTER SIX

SPRING AGAIN

But at last, the yearly miracle happened, the grass grew, the swallows swooped, the cuckoo called and the trees donned their gorgeous greenery. My spirits rose accordingly and I felt an air of confidence as we prepared to repeat last year's jobs of planting, hoeing and such like. Potatoes are usually the first crop to be tilled, but first we had to open the clamp to get our seeds. But, along with the other workers, a new face appeared, Ben arrived.

I don't think that I have yet mentioned that my employer and his wife belonged to a very strict religious sect called The Plymouth

Brethren, about as straight laced as one could get. Even a radio was considered a 'worldly thing' and therefore sinful, so they had none, but the boss would enquire of us the latest news during any particular crisis on the war front.

The women all had long hair and although they had no church, they met regularly for prayer and worship. People came to stay at the farm from time to time, but they were always of the same close society, and I believe Ben's parents had sent their son to the farm to maybe help out a bit and learn something about the land as well. Anyway, he was a typical lively seventeen-year-old, full of fun and *joie de vivre*, and to me, he was like a breath of fresh air, we were instant friends.

We all set to and started work on the spuds, sorting them roughly into three types, those fit for human consumption, those suitable for seed and the rejects, small ones or ones that had become dry and wizened and a few which had rotted and produced a dreadful stink were tossed aside. We knelt on folded sacks as we did the sorting and took a perverse delight in placing a squashy, smelly potato on others' kneeling pads when they rose to empty the bucket or mawn, into the sacks.

Occasionally Ben and I were left to get on with it, and then the fun really began — rotten potatoes flying around and howls of rage when they found their target — even the pungent smell of the rotten spuds couldn't subdue our lively spirits.

Then another job came along, not any fun at all, this one in a small shed at the bottom of the yard, where quicklime had been stored during the winter. This was now needed on the land, and had to be loaded onto the butt and hauled out. Alas! the paper sacks, each containing 1 cwt, had split and now it all had to be re-bagged into sound sacks. Ben and I were given the job, and I held the sacks open whilst Ben shovelled it in with a fire pan. In the thick atmosphere, our exuberance soon evaporated, we could scarcely see each other through the thick pall of lime dust, and we emerged looking a whiter shade of pale! I helped him load it, then I did other odd jobs till he returned for more and then we had to re-enter the torture chamber. I found an old udder cloth that I tied over my nose and mouth, but Ben didn't bother with that, I think he was past caring. It took several days to clear the shed, Ben confided in me that at leave work time, the lady of the house had insisted that he removed all his clothes, down to his underpants, outside, to reduce the risk of

16

bringing too much lime inside.

At least he was able to take a bath, not many houses boasted a bathroom in the forties, especially in the country. My face, hands and forearms were burned, but Ben's back and shoulders were nearly raw with humping the sacks off the butt. I felt so sorry for him, he was only a boy, younger than I was, and far from home. Not long after that, Ben went as abruptly as he came, and who could blame him!

But now another job came my way that I did really enjoy. Petrol rationing had become tighter so the boss decided that the milk he bought from two farms in the area, would have to be fetched back by horse power, instead of using a car. So every morning my first job was to put Punch into the butt and go first to Kennerland and then to Lane Barton to collect it.

Now this was a piece of cake. I stood up at the front end of the butt, and was able to look over the hedges and see what was happening in the fields; whose potatoes were planted; where the first corn fields were beginning to show a pale green sheen; wonder why farmer X hadn't spread that heap of muck yet. There was always someone at the farms to give me a helping hand to load the churns and I got a cheery greeting too, and a dear old soul who lived beside the road would rush out when she heard the horse's footsteps and thrust a thick slice of bread, spread with syrup and cream into my hand. I suppose it must have rained some days but in my imagination, I can feel that warmth of the sun on my bare arms, and the smell of wild roses and honeysuckle on the breeze. Surely one of my happier memories.

Now the cows and young stock were out in the field enjoying the lush spring grass, and it was good to be alive. I had more or less forgotten my grievances of the previous winter when something else happened that clinched my determination to move to another farm. I had been sent out to pick up stones, so, armed with a bucket and *that* wheelbarrow, I set off. I gathered the stones into the bucket, tipped them into the barrow, which, when full, I wheeled to the corner of the field and tipped the contents into a pile.

I rather liked working on my own sometimes, it gave me time to think and enjoy my own company. I think I've always been a bit of a loner. People talk of loneliness, but for my part, I don't experience it. Anyway, I was happily plodding on with my work when I became aware of the boss standing at the top of the field where some vegetables had been tilled. I didn't give it much thought, but then he came over and, pulling out a large pocket watch, informed me that I had taken half an hour to fill the barrow, whereas he had done it easily the previous evening in twenty five minutes. I straightened up and looked at him, lost for words, nails ingrained with soil, back aching, and a wave of different emotions swept over me. Anger first because I felt it was unjust and astonishment that he could do such a thing to me. I had been there over a year and had given everything I had to whatever job I was doing. All I could bring myself to say was, "I'm doing my best," and he walked away. Reg, my boyfriend, was furious. It was common knowledge amongst the workers, that the boss used a powerful pair of binoculars to check on us when we were in the fields, and he was good at appearing, not through the gate, but through a gap in the hedge, to take us unawares. I decided this was the last straw, but I would keep quiet and look for a change of employer.

A short while after this, Doris, the other girl who lived in, had her father and younger brother come to stay. Doris had the retail milk round, taking in Bucks Cross and Bucks Mills. I don't think these two visitors belonged to the Brethren because Doris had been converted to it since working at Alminstone. The milk was loaded, all bottled up and in crates, on to a little donkey cart pulled by a good natured cob. Now the shafts of this small cart had an important item missing, there were no chains to which the breeching could be attached and which prevented the cart slipping forward on a downward slope. Without it, the cart could end up with the front resting against the horse's rear end.

Well, it's pretty steep, that road down to Bucks Mills, Doris' dad decided to go with his daughter on the round, and was horrified when he saw the state of the cart, and the risks involved. He told the boss in no uncertain language that no way was Doris going to use that cart again until it was brought up to scratch. I expect Doris stood meekly by during the confrontation, but it did the trick, for the time being anyway, and the milk was delivered by car. But just as soon as Dad returned to London, Doris was back using the cart again. I never knew if it ever got fixed.

The brother, by the name of John, stayed on for a while longer. He was a lanky, rather gormless lad, and I mostly ignored him. However, John and I did share, with retrospect, one rather amusing experience. The boss had taken some grass keep about six miles

18

away, beyond Thornhill Head. Some dry cows had been put on this land to eat the grass and Mr Norris used to drive out there every day to check they were OK. One morning he told John and me to get into the car and go to these fields with him, where he would part out some of the cows that were close to calving and John and I were to take them back to the farm where they would be under closer surveillance. We were delighted, trying hard not to show it, because it sounded a cushy job — a ride in a car and a leisurely amble back home. Little did we think what lay in store — those cows had other ideas. Together we picked out four or five cows, and the boss set us on our way, then went off leaving us to do the droving. At first, all went well, they were heavily pregnant so not to be rushed, and it was a very hot day.

Our troubles began when we reached the unfenced moor. The slogan was "Dig for Victory", and the gorse, brambles and heather that usually grew on such land, had been all cleared away, the land ploughed and a flourishing crop of potatoes had replaced the natural scrub. Once the cows noticed that there was no fence, the temptation to investigate proved irresistible. The low bank was no obstacle, they piled over it, and ran amok amongst the spuds.

Now I can assure you, it was not an easy exercise to run around in a patch of healthy potatoes, at least for mere mortals. The cows had no such problems, admittedly their legs were longer than ours, and they had four each as opposed to our two. I yelled instructions to John, he yelled back and mayhem resulted. It seemed ages, and probably was, before we go those recalcitrant creatures back onto the road and heading in the right direction. In those conditions, with the sun at full strength, we were both utterly exhausted by our efforts. What the owner of the potato crop thought when he surveyed the damage, I shudder to think. We certainly didn't hang around to find out! We were perspiring like racehorses and so thirsty we could only croak at one another.

We must have looked an odd pair as we trudged along behind the now docile animals, the pale, skinny boy from the city and the sun tanned girl of the land. We peered into the ditches in search of water but they had all dried up. Then an oasis appeared, in the form of a milk stand, upon which were half a dozen churns, and it was no mirage. John and I noticed it at the same moment and simultaneously the same idea came to us. Like a pair of homing pigeons, we leapt on to that stand in one bound and felt the churns. Joy of joys! they had milk in them! We raised a lid, tilted the churn so that milk flowed into it, and drank until our thirst was quenched. The poor old farmer lost a bit from his milk cheque that day, but I feel sure he would not have begrudged it to us.

The rest of the journey was free from problems, we didn't tell the boss about the cows' bad behaviour, he would probably have worked out that we were to blame, anyhow. Soon after that, John too went back to the city, but I feel sure he would recall that incident if he is still alive.

CHAPTER SEVEN

MY HOME FROM HOME

My change of jobs came about in a roundabout way, but before I go into all that, this seems a good moment to pause awhile and tell, in more detail, about my life in digs.

Emily and her husband Bill, had a small County Council holding on which they grew the obligatory potatoes, mangolds, and swedes. They also kept a few milking cows, some beef cattle, a flock of hens and two horses. There were two young sons, John and Ken aged about eight and six when I first went there. Emily also had her elderly father living there; he was quite sweet under a forbidding exterior, and we got along fine. He would enquire what I had been doing, and offer little tips and advice. The children were no problem either, being friendly and reasonably well-behaved, and I became very fond of them. We ran races together, played cricket and football in the fields, and I taught them some games from my childhood. I helped look after the frogs' spawn that we kept in 2 lb jam jars, and their collection of birds' eggs, but they had their own code of conduct, and only took one egg from a nest. I suppose I became a sort of older sister to them.

The house was the usual small farm type and in the kitchen was a large black range, which was lit at weekends to heat the water for the baths, and to roast the Sunday meat. In the back kitchen was a white porcelain sink, and the best feature was the open-fireplace. A huge log was at the back, and smaller logs were placed against it to create a good fire. The back-stick never really went out, a few dry kindlings in the morning, a puff or two from the bellows, and one was away. We dried our boots and coats before it each night. Black kettles and pots hung from chains and crooks above the blaze, and an iron trivet or tripod enabled vegetables to be boiled, or a stew cooked over the heat. We huddled around its warmth with gratitude.

In a corner, next to the open fireplace, was the copper. This was a very large copper container, with a wooden lid, which was positioned over a fireplace, the smoke from which entered the big open chimney higher up. The clothes were boiled up in this apparatus, and clouds of steam filled the kitchen. Washing day really took a whole day, as the white things were washed first, followed by the colours, and lastly the rough clothes were scrubbed on the long wooden seat, or form, taken out into the yard, after which the table and form were scrubbed off, and the kitchen floor washed. Quite a day!

On the other side of the fire stood an oil cooker which had a ring and an oven. The oil containers, or fountains, were inverted over pipes that carried the oil to the burners. On this strange piece of equipment Emily would produce mouth-watering cut-rounds and yeast cake, also sponge cakes as light as feathers. How clever she was not only in her culinary skill, but also in the way she was able to stretch the meagre rations so that we were never hungry.

Saturday night was bath-night. The bath was a long, tin affair, called a bungalow bath, and it was fetched in from an outhouse, and placed before the black range, or bodly. The two boys were bathed first, then it was my turn, after some more hot water had been added. Being very shy, I was very fussy about making sure the curtains were closely pulled, but the boys took a delight in telling me they had been able to peep through a chink I hadn't noticed. I didn't really believe them, but took more care the following week to get the blackout secure! Someone had given me some bath-salts — luxury indeed! but after a few weeks we discovered that they were causing the bath to rust, so that was the end of that!

There were three tabby cats, and they were good mousers, and caught the occasional rat too. The children made a fuss of them, and they came in by day but were always put out at night. My room had a window directly above the front porch and one night I was awakened by the feeling of something moving on my bed. I put out my hand and encountered this furry object. Suppressing a scream that would have woken the whole household, I fumbled for my torch and recognized the intruder — a cat! It must have leapt from the front gate, on to the porch, where one more bound took it through my open window. I made sure that I opened the other window after that.

On one occasion, my supervisor called by to ask me if I would visit another land-girl, who had recently arrived on a farm near by. This girl was from the city and very, very home-sick. Maybe it would cheer her up a bit to get a call from another land-girl. Although I had never been to this farm, I knew where it was, and John said he would go with me. It was mid-winter, and as dark as pitch when we set off on our mission. We had one small torch, with a weak battery, so that had to be nursed and only used in an emergency. It was a long lane and we couldn't see a thing, but held hands to give each other confidence. It seemed to go on for ever, but at last a faint chink of light told us we had arrived. A knock on the door, and in we went, into the biggest kitchen I have ever seen. Blue-flagstones on the floor, a huge open fireplace at one end, and along one wall a table that probably twenty people could have sat round. I heard afterwards that the horse came right into that room, pulling the back-stick for the open fire. Seated beside the fire was this young girl, and I could tell at a glance that she wasn't Land Army material. She looked pale and delicate and had been crying. I did all I could to encourage her, telling her that winter would pass, and how lovely the spring would be, but I could see I was not making much headway. Nothing I could say, or the amusing prattle of the two little girls playing on the floor raised even a hint of a smile, and shortly after that, she left. John and I, like horses, seemed to get home much quicker than the outward trip, and a cup of hot cocoa in front of the fire soon put us in good spirits again. I suspect that this sort of situation arose many times, as city-bred girls with a 'picture postcard' idea of life down on the farm, found it far different when faced with stark reality. But for all that, many girls got stuck in, and became great assets to the depleted labour force.

How simple and uncomplicated life was! The long dark evenings never bothered me then, I wrote lots of letters, read the paper from end to end, and helped amuse the boys. A local small-holder cut hair, and Emily and I, and the boys would regularly go to get ourselves tidied up. I believe we paid 6d. each, but it was a social event, as Mary, the barber's wife, and Emily gossiped, and we all chattered away like magpies — it was a full evening's entertainment.

I was happy to do jobs around the house, washing dishes, doing some dusting or scrubbing the floor, and I regularly turned the handle of the mangle — a wonderful contraption that reduced the pile of ironing no end. Emily was so good to me, I just wanted to show some appreciation. Food of course was strictly rationed, but in the country we fared better than the town and city dwellers. We had eggs, plenty of milk, an occasional fowl, fresh vegetables and twice a year a pig was slaughtered for the table. In those days, before freezers came into use, the meat all had to be salted and stored in large earthenware pans, called trendles.

But a sort of system had been thought up whereby neighbours were given pieces of fresh pork, and when they killed their pig, they gave us a similar piece in return. The salted meat would keep for months although the last few pieces would get pretty salty, it was true. The old rule of thumb was, only to kill a pig when there was an 'R' in the month, i.e., from September to April, because during the other months flies would be a problem. Emily made the most delicious hogs puddings. I can still smell the aroma that drifted from the heavy frying pan as the pudding was frying, and how we all gobbled it up with gusto. No factory made product could ever compare with it, it was fit for a king.

During the summer, we would occasionally go to Bucks Mills on a Sunday. We went on our bicycles and of course, took food and drink. Usually we left our bikes at Bucks Cross, the long haul up from the beach meant we couldn't ride them anyway. The boys had a right good time on those outings, paddling in the sea, searching the rock pools or playing about with a ball. I would spend most of the time with them, but always had a good swim before we ate our picnic. Then the breathtaking walk back up the hill, and a two mile cycle ride to get back home, but we never doubted it was all well worth the effort. Sometimes we took a picnic down to the river and this too was a lovely treat, the water was crystal clear and pollution free. We paddled and caught minnows, ran races and skimmed stones.

The water meadows had a profusion of wild flowers, clover, buttercups and meadow sweet grew alongside the reeds and bulrushes. These little outings cost nothing in terms of money, but they provided so much pleasure. Today, children with TV and videos are missing out on the best things in life. A day out now probably means a costly visit to a theme park or the like, and they would probably find it hard to accept that we had so much pleasure from such simple things.

There were exciting moments too. A neighbour's young son, about three years my junior, had acquired a spirited young horse which he planned to ride in local point-to-point events and gymkhanas. I had ridden a bit as a child, nothing very polished about my skill, I knew how to get on and off the beast, and stay on board most of the time anyway. Well, one evening he came by, on his horse, to show it to us. We all gathered round and admired it, for truth to tell, it was a smart looking animal. Suddenly he looked at me and asked if I would like to ride it. I wasn't too eager as I could see it was a bit headstrong, but I wasn't going to look a coward in front of the little group, so up I got.

I trotted over to the crossways and then proceeded up the hill and my confidence grew by the minute — I was enjoying this! Thinking it was about time I returned the horse to its owner, I turned round and started the short ride back. Whether something frightened the brute, or he suddenly became possessed by an evil spirit I never knew, but he bolted. No amount of whoas! or pulling on the reins had any effect. The little crowd standing round scattered, they probably sensed something was not right, as I flashed past clinging on for grim life. Up the lane we flew, like greased lightning and into the yard. Now at the far end was a closed gate and we were heading straight for it. Either I was going to be catapulted over its head or it was going to jump the gate, in which case, I'd come off anyhow.

But neither of these things happened, seeing the obstacle way ahead, my mount wheeled round and came to a halt. The sweat was in flecks on his neck and flanks, but all the steam had gone out of him and he trotted nicely back down the lane, where I met the owner and the onlookers, coming to see what had happened. I slid gratefully to the ground, handed the reins over to the lad and said with as much aplomb as I could muster, "He's a good mover," and assured my anxious audience that they should not have worried on my account. They didn't pursue the matter, but I guess they suspected that it wasn't quite like I made it out to be and I never got offered a second ride! The horse did quite well at point-to-point races, until it threw its rider, resulting in a broken arm.

On Sundays, I went to the Methodist Chapel, one hundred yards over the road, and was warmly welcomed. Usually there was a good congregation, several of the farmers and business folk had cars although one farmer and his wife arrived in a pony and trap — usually late!

There was strict petrol rationing, but there was an allowance to enable people to attend a place of worship. I guess that nearly everyone claimed to be church goers, just to get the extra petrol. But to justify a visit, to family or friends, people only had to put a sack of potatoes or turnips in the back seat and they felt covered. As usual, there are loopholes for any rule or regulation.

On Sunday we always had a roast dinner, the joints were so small because of rationing, it was impossible to recognize which part of the carcase they came from. So, inevitably, sometimes our roast meat would have been more suited to an hour or so in the pot. When the meat was put on our plates, if we had difficulty in cutting it up with our usual dinner knives, a sharp butchers knife was passed around so that we could deal with it more easily. Can't remember anyone complaining of indigestion either!

The sweet was always junket during the summer and delicious it was too. To give it its special flavour, it needed some nutmeg. One didn't buy it all ground in little drums then, oh! no, the whole nutmegs had to be dealt with, by using a grater; the boys loved this job for some reason, and argued as to who should do it. The younger lad quite often let the nutmeg fall, plop! into the junket, from where it had to be fetched out with a spoon. This always incurred his father's wrath. I used to have to turn away to hide my smiles as I thought it rather funny.

It was almost impossible to buy a watch or clock during the war, but Emily had a lovely wall clock that kept good time and which hung on the kitchen wall. Now I did have a pocket watch that my brother had given me, which rested in my pocket and was secured by a length of cord to my belt. Somewhere along the line it had lost its minute hand, but the hour hand was OK so I could calculate the time to within a few minutes.

My biggest worry during the winter was that I would oversleep and be late for work. I had a small torch under my pillow, but when I consulted my watch on one particular morning, it had stopped. There was only one way of finding out exactly what the time was and that was to go downstairs and consult the big clock. Sliding out of my warm bed, I slipped downstairs, the tiny torch just about showing me the way.

As I stepped off the last stair, what a shock! I found myself ankle deep in icy water. Heavy rain had fallen during the night pouring down the hill and under the front door, so that the little hall was about three inches under water. As it happened, it was too early to get up but I fetched everyone's wellies to the foot of the stairs so they didn't get a similar shock. They were most grateful and I earned a clutch of brownie points for that good deed.

Of course, we had no electricity or running water, and lights were fuelled by oil, and we used candles to go to bed. A lead pump in the kitchen provided lovely drinking water. We were luckier than most because we have a lavatory outside the back door, not at the bottom of the garden and it had an overhead tank which meant that it could be flushed.

I became friendly with another land girl from a neighbouring farm and we used to go to Church parades and rallies together. These get-togethers could be anywhere in the region, but were mostly held in the Exeter area. We would be taken there by our supervisor, a sweet, kindly lady from Bideford.

Doreen was a happy, lively girl, she knew little of the country way of life till she came to Devon, but now she could feed calves, milk, and do other jobs around the farm. But she was having a problem with her widowed mother who was constantly pleading with her to go back nearer to London. Doreen was her only child and eventually she weakened. I was so sorry to see her go, but we never lost touch and have visited each other over the years; two of her children used to come to stay with us on the farm, and now she too is a widow.

CHAPTER EIGHT

SOCIAL LIFE

You might think that fifty years ago or more, in the middle of a war, we had a pretty dull life. No electricity, television sets almost unheard of, a strict blackout in force, no transport other than our trusty bikes, just what was there to do? Well, the radio was our main source of amusement and we all gathered around to hear our favourite programmes, such as I.T.M.A., Up the Pole, Dick Barton Special Agent, and lots of special efforts were made from time-to-time to raise money for the war effort. The village school master, Mr Griffiths, and his wife were absolutely wizard at organizing such events and teaching the children stirring, patriotic songs, many of which he composed himself. Of course, we went to all these events, partly because they were special and partly because they gave us an excuse to get out for a few hours.

During the summer months, Reg and I had two evenings out per week, Sunday and Wednesday, and I had to be back in by 10.00 p.m. That is, unless there was a dance at the village hall, these were star attractions, quite often there was a whist drive, before the dance, and we all enjoyed that of course, the prizes were trifling, a packet of cigs or half a dozen eggs, so nobody got up tight at their partners' occasional mistake. Then at around 9.30 p.m. the tables were cleared, and the Woolsery Band arrived. This consisted of a set of drums, a guitar and a piano accordion. We thought the music grand — it was too, and we pranced around doing the Lambeth Walk, the Okey Cokey and whirled around like dervishes for the quick step, but became more sedate for the last waltz. Talcum powder was sprinkled over the floor in an effort to give it a bit of a slip, but on a wet night it was a losing battle, as the door opened straight onto the street, and so people came in with wet coats and feet. At around 11.00 p.m. there was a break for refreshments, how these were produced in those days of ration books and shortages, I'll never know, but there was always a selection to choose from. I seem to recall that the cost of a ticket for the whist drive and dance, plus the food, was about half a crown, today's 12½ pence! All of us arrived on bicycles, many without either a front or rear light and these were dumped in the farmer's shed opposite the hall. No fears then that they might be stolen. We talked about our night out for days afterwards, and there was much speculation as to which lad had taken which girl home. We certainly had our moneys' worth.

Cards was also a favourite past time, we played Nap and Newmarket mainly, and occasionally had a mild flutter on them, never more than tuppence on Newmarket, or sixpence on Nap, but usually we just played for fun — or matches! and people seemed to drop in, to discuss the price of pigs, the quality of the neighbours hay, or who was on the move come Lady Day. There was always a cup of tea before they left for home. We were so pleased with what, today, would seem pretty second rate entertainment. Maybe the war, even so far removed from it as we were, bonded us all together.

CHAPTER NINE

THE MOVE AND NEW JOBS

When Doreen left, this opened the door of opportunity I had been looking for. I jumped on my bike and went to see the farmer who had been employing her. He seemed quite keen to take me on, and although I had not done much milking, I was eager to learn. I already knew him and his wife slightly, through the Chapel, in fact Mr Lott was a local preacher.

Any change of employment was supposed to be done through the official channels, and fortunately it was approved. I gave my boss two weeks' notice, and left without a trace of regret, and in fact, it was the best thing that could have happened. I was still in the same locality, I could stay in the same digs and still have my boy-friend near by. I found my new boss friendly and helpful and his wife another dear soul. Very soon I was introduced to the dairy cows and the mysteries of the milking machine.

So began my life-long love affair with cows, and I was never happier than when I was left alone to get on with the milking. The cows were mostly Shorthorns, and some pedigree cows in the herd. Pedigree status was then another mystery to me, they seemed to look just the same as the others, and didn't give any more milk either — I was not very impressed. One shippon held fifteen cows, another twenty and part of the stable block accommodated five. The fifteen cow shed was quite modern with the advantage of a walk-way in front of the cows which made it much easier to feed them their hay and roots. The floors were of concrete and the walls were plastered smoothly to a height of about five feet so that they could be kept clean, a damp day was ideal for this job, and made the scrubbing off of any muck a lot easier.

All this had to be done to qualify for the extra payment that milk from a TT-tested Herd earned. When I say I milked alone, this was not strictly true. Yes, I operated the Alfa-Laval bucket type machine, but after the cluster was removed, Bert, the same man who did a lot of work with the cows, used to sit down on a three legged stool, and with a hooded bucket strip out any milk remaining in the udder. This was a procedure, long since outdated, of getting the very last few drops, after the cluster was taken off. He grumbled a lot if there was more than half a cupful. Now my boss had impressed upon me the need to keep the machines moving along, so when I told him about the man's complaints, he merely told me to ignore them.

From time-to-time a man arrived in a little Austin eight car, and he was employed by the Milk Marketing Board to weigh and record the milk each cow gave, but no samples were taken. We tipped the milk from the machine bucket into a stainless steel pail, and this was hung on a clock faced balance which hung from a crook in the ceiling.

We were always glad when we had got that over and done with. I wonder if today farmers feel the same about their recording? In those days, if a cow produced five gallons, i.e., twenty two litres, she was very good. Now forty litres per day is quite common, fifty litres or more not unheard of and I even recorded sixty litres, given over two milkings — but only once. I got used to doing the afternoon milking, and did the morning milking when I was needed.

At my new farm, I came upon a hitherto unknown crop — kale. The cows loved it and as no one had invented the electric fencer yet, it had to be cut, and taken out to the field and tossed out of the cart, with the horse in motion, so that the cattle all got an equal chance to eat it. I was taken to the field, given a hook that had been shortened, till it looked a bit like a long heavy knife, and shown how to cut the stalks, and then of course they had to be loaded on the cart. The horse was called Tommy. He was a good natured animal, if a bit gormless, but he never bit or even showed his teeth and I could harness him up and tackle him into the cart with no fears at all. Whilst I was cutting the load, I tied Tommy loosely to the hedge until I was ready to load.

This worked very well, till one day Tommy got away from his flimsy restraint and went walk-about along the hedge looking for tastier morsels. It so happened my lunch-bag was hooked over a stump in the hedge, some distance from where Tommy had been left, but alas, when I went to have my elevenses prior to loading the kale, Tommy had pulled it from the hedge and trodden on it. The flask was crushed flat, and my bits of bread and cheese and currant roll were saturated in tea. I went hungry till dinner-time that day, but realized I couldn't really blame the horse! As the winter closed in, many mornings the kale would be white with hoar-frost, which reduced my hands to blocks of ice, and the kale was always wet. On one occasion, it was a lovely day, and I felt happy with life and as

29

I tossed the kale out over the side, I burst into song. Now I don't know whether it took Tommy by surprise or what, but he stopped dead in his tracks. Taken unawares, I was thrown over the side and landed heavily in the field. Afraid someone might have seen my embarrassment, I was soon back on board. Actually I put him to the test after that, and yes, if I started to sing, he'd stop. Was it really that awful?

Sometimes, Bert and I were sent out hedging. He took such a pride in his work, I was only his skivvy, and the only jobs I was allowed to do, was to heave up the 'filling', or to foot out the bottom with a mattock. But his enthusiasm was infectious, and I became really fond of the job.

On one occasion, on a Saturday, it was his usual half-day, and he was put out hedging in the morning. He came back into the yard at 2.15 as apparently he was so wrapped up in the job in hand that he didn't realize how the time was going!

I spent a lot of time in the cowsheds cleaning and washing out. We also kept the walls scrubbed, and cob-webs swept away. The troughs also got cleaned out every day and scrubbed once a week. The dairy was dominated by the milk cooler. The milk was tipped into a big receiver tank, and the tap turned on, when the milk flowed down over a ripple surface cooler, and then into churns underneath. Water passed through this device and it did a remarkably efficient job. The worst thing that could happen was to forget to change the churns, so that there was an overflow on to the floor. Even my good-tempered boss was cross then, and I felt he was justified.

I also fed the calves, and took delight in seeing them grow. But I found that their teeth were very sharp and my fingers usually had cuts on them. One calf was particularly good at finger biting, and I hit on a good idea to protect my middle finger. I wrapped some old rag round it, and yes, all was well. The calf still suckled well, but as it slurped up the last dregs, the rag came off and slipped down its throat. I was horrified; it was a pedigree calf, and I dreaded what damage the rag might cause — stoppage or violent stomach upset? It was with a very anxious heart I reported for work the next morning, but the calf was bright as a button. I never tried that trick again, but let my fingers get chewed up instead.

As the Spring approached, so life on the farm took on a faster tempo. There were so many jobs all crying out to be done; potatoes to plant; grass ground to chain-harrow and roll, and the cattle houses to be cleaned out. As the winter progressed, the young stock that were housed loose in various sheds, had fresh straw bedding put in every day to keep them warm and as dry as possible. By the end of winter, this had built up to a compacted mass, sometimes a quarter or a third of the way up the walls, and often the cattle knelt to eat the corn that was put into the feed troughs, as these were only just above the level of the manure. The cattle in these sheds were let out into the yard, and we set to with a fork to heave the muck out, sometimes through the open door, and sometimes through a window.

It was hard work indeed, the easiest way was to sort of peel it off in layers. The stench was pretty strong, but the curious thing was, that in a short while, we could not smell it much, but it clung to our hair and clothes and everyone else could tell what our job had been! The feeling of achievement when one finally found the cobbled stone floor at the bottom! The men spat into their hands but I never copied them although I could see the reasoning behind it, and hard galls appeared at the base of my fingers. There was corn to be tilled, but before that, there had to be a threshing day.

CHAPTER TEN

THRESHING DAY

A local man with a threshing machine and a steam engine to provide power to work it, used to go around the neighbourhood and perform the useful service. To keep the furnace going, one had to have a supply of steam coal, and plenty of water available for the boiler. These magnificent machines were looked after with loving care by their owners. The brass plates shone like mirrors, and oily rags were used to keep their black bodies spick and span.

Now threshing needed a lot of hands, and much the same system worked as with the potato harvest. One borrowed staff from neighbouring farms, and one had to help them out when they threshed. It was a recognized thing that all food was provided for the eight or ten men on those days, and a special food allowance was available to enable the farmer's wife to do this. So, the day before, there was a huge cook-up in the farm kitchen — cut-rounds, yeast-cake, pasties and tarts to feed the men, who would always be hungry,

31

as threshing was hard work indeed.

The owner of the machine would arrive early on the day, to get the fire going and the steam up. He and his father would be given breakfast. At around 11 a.m. food and drink would be taken to the workers. Bread and cheese and cake, and copious amounts of tea, which was usually carried in a tall white enamelled jug. The food was put in a large, flat-bottomed basket, known as a butter-basket, and covered with a white cloth. This break lasted about ten minutes. The farmer's wife then gathered up her — by now, empty basket and jugs, and we got back to work.

Dinner-time, we all flocked into the farmhouse kitchen, where quite often it was roast pork on the menu, from a recent slaughter, with apple pie and cream to follow, washed down with yet more tea. Nothing the Dorchester offered could have tasted better. We wolfed it down amid general good humour and farm talk, then there was a scraping of chairs, a heartfelt thank you to the farmer's wife and back on the job. Usually, we had tea as well, the inevitable "teddy" pasty, apple tart, and yeast buns. Very little notice was paid to what time we finished, we just plodded on till the job was done.

Now to some explanation of what the actual work entailed. If the corn was in a Dutch barn, that was one problem solved, in that it was under cover so no early morning decision had to be taken, as to whether it was safe to strip the thatch. An outside rick would have been thatched, soon after harvest, with rushes cut from a nearby marsh, held down with thatching rope and spars.

That was a specialist job, and looked great when properly done, with large stones tied along the eaves to prevent the thatch lifting in the winter storms. But, all being prepared, the big machine fixed alongside the rick, work began. There were two men on the machine, usually the owner Bill and his son George, one cut the "beans", the binder cord that tied the sheaf, and the other "fed" it into the drum. Very occasionally, the knife would go into the drum along with the corn sheaf, a nasty grating noise accompanied by the muttered curses of the cutter would tell us what had happened, it was farewell to a good knife. Two of us were on the rick, pitching the corn up to the platform, and the sheaves had to be sent up in the correct way, not just in untidy bundles, with butts and ears together. At first it was comparatively easy, but as the rick sank, so it got progressively more difficult to pitch the sheaves higher, and the aim was to keep the men on the thresher busy non-stop.

Dust was everywhere — thick clouds of it — and also the chaff flew about in the wind. We were sweating, and it stuck to us, and slipped down our shirts, but there was a sense of team-work which gave it a great measure of enjoyment. Usually there were four spouts at one end of the thresher where the corn came out, and these could be shut off, so that one used two at a time. The good corn ran out of one spout, and the poor stuff out of the other. There were strong iron hooks on which to hang the bags. When the bag became full, the shutter on that spout was closed and the other opened, so that there was no hold-up whilst bags were changed over. It took a strong man to carry the full sacks of corn away, and invariably they had to be carried up the granary steps, and tipped into the grain hoppers, which had all been carefully swept clean to take the new supply. My boss had a gadget to help the man carrying the sacks, to get it on his back. The full bag was placed on a platform of iron bars, which was in a big frame, with a handle at one side. This handle, when turned, hoisted the sack up so that it was easier to transfer to one's back. A simple release lever allowed the platform to slide back to ground level, ready for the next sack. One had to keep one's wits about one, to 'mind' the corn, as an overfull bag, or worse still, spilt grain was not appreciated, and without the hoisting machine, it was the job of the corn minder to help raise the sack on to the carrier's back. The truss was at the other end of the thresher, and this dealt with the straw, which came out of its depths, as tied-up bundles or wads as they were called. These were tied in two places with binder twine, and were immediately taken away, either by horse and cart to be stacked away in tallets, a sort of attic above a stable or bullocks' shed, or a rick was made close at hand. As well as the wads of straw, small bits of broken straw, and the husks of the actual seeds of corn came out, and a huge heap of chaff mounted up, which had to be scooped away from time to time, otherwise the man on the trusser would have been buried. As the rick got lower and lower, rats that had made their winter quarters in it, began to run out. Now I was absolutely petrified by rats (I still am) and had been told so many horror stories about rats having run up trouser legs, that I dreaded the last few layers of the rick. However, I had been advised to tie some twine around the bottom of my dungaree legs, which was some comfort. The War-Ag, as we called them, decided that rats were doing a lot of damage and eating a lot of grain, so it became law to fence in the whole threshing area with fine-mesh netting, to prevent the vermin escaping and the neighbours round about brought their terriers and lurchers to put a speedy end to the fugitives.

At last, it was done, we eased up our aching backs, ruefully surveyed our blistered hands, and decided it had been a good day. The topic amongst the neighbours for days after would be the thresh, how the corn had run, the quality of the straw and the number of rats accounted for. It was all discussed at great length. So, now the seed corn was ready to plant, but the fields allocated for corn-crops had yet to be made ready.

CHAPTER ELEVEN

SEED TIME

Through the winter, weather permitting, the land had been ploughed. This had been done by my boss, and, wonder of wonders, he had a tractor! It was what was known as a row-crop model, the two front wheels being quite close together. It was a big, yellow monster, from America, a Minneapolis Moline, or M.M. for short. It ran on T.V.O., but had to be started on petrol.

Before too long, I was introduced to its mysteries, and I remember I felt very important indeed when I was first perched up on its uncomfortable metal seat. The noise it made was pretty loud, and blotted out every other sound. More of that later. One of the workmen, called Bill, was generally in charge of the horses, and so the job of spreading fertiliser, lime and slag fell to him. We loaded up the butt, and I drove the horse up and down the fields at a measured distance from the previous wheel-marks, whilst he flung the fertiliser out over the land with either a firepan, or a tin plate, such as pasties were baked on.

The fertiliser wasn't too bad to deal with, but lime and slag, particularly the latter, were not much fun. Slag was black/grey in colour, and any rogue gust of wind would send the stuff all over us. At first, his blackened face amused me, until I realized that mine was just the same. It was fatal to try and wash it off, the secret was to have a rag, and wipe off as much as one could before washing. Sometimes he miscalculated how fast he was getting rid of the stuff, and we had to return to the barn for more. At other times we had some left after the field had been gone over, that wasn't so bad, as he just chucked it out at random to get rid of it — doesn't sound very technical now, does it? Then the fields had to be worked down, that is, a good tilth produced to receive the seed. As a rule, it first had a going over with a heavy roller, pulled by the M.M. Then it probably needed two or three passes with the tine harrows, often done by horse power, the set of three being attached to a draught, then hooked up to the long chains that were attached to the horses harness. I enjoyed this, yes, it did make one footsore, but the best of it was, one could look around, and also hear the birds' song whilst following the horse. At last, it was ready, and the corn was taken to the field and the horse hitched into the corn-drill — a long box on wheels — from which the seed ran down to the coulters, which in turn let the seed fall in very shallow troughs in the soil. If it was horse-drawn, one man could operate it, but if tractor-drawn, someone had to ride the corn-drill, to check that the seed was running properly, and also to spot when more seed had to be tipped into the box. I was never allowed to drill corn on my own, but did ride the corn-drill, and another duty was to raise the box at the ends, so as not to over-drill. As a matter of fact, I never wanted to drill a field of corn on my own, because, about ten days or so later when the seeds started to come up, any errors made were there for all to see. A wide bare space indicated that the machine had been 'under-driven', thicker rows showed where the opposite had occurred, and, worst of all, a bare patch showed where either a chokeage had happened, or the seed had been allowed to run out. And of course, there was no way these defects could be hidden, they were there in full view, and one had to run the gauntlet of the neighbours' caustic remarks. Sometimes, a few days after the corn was tilled, grass seeds would be sown in the same field, so that, after corn-harvest, there was a field of young grass, all tilled and ready for another spring, or to provide a tasty bite for sheep and lambs. When the gate was closed, all that man could do, had been done. Now it was up to Mother Nature.

The cows had been tied up by the neck in the shippens for several months, occasionally, weather permitting, they were let out into the yard to scratch and stretch their legs, that was all. The poor creatures became wildly excited as they went into the field, where luscious grass was 2/3 inches high, and they went berserk, charging around the field, bucking their legs in the air, just like spring lambs.

Finally they would settle down and begin to enjoy their food, and we waited with eager anticipation for the milk yield to rise — which it always did. I took a great interest in the amount of milk produced, and one day the boss said that, if I liked, he would pay me a bonus on the milk produced, instead of overtime (yes! we did get extra pay for extra work at that farm!)

I thought a lot about the offer, but turned it down, as I didn't want my concern about how much milk was sold, to be related to money, so I explained this to the boss. He didn't pass any comment, but smiled in a sort of special way, so I think he understood.

When we put out the young stock a bit later on, they were far worse than the cows. The sheds in which they were wintered were dark, and the poor creatures could barely see when the doors were opened, and walked into walls and each other. They had to be gradually introduced to bright spring sunshine, and spent several days in a yard, a bit longer each day, till we felt they were acclimatized. But even so, they too careered madly round the fields and it took several hours before they settled down.

CHAPTER TWELVE

HAYMAKING

Meanwhile, the corn was growing well, but so, too, were the weeds. There were no sprays in those days of course, so in about mid May, corn weeding began. We all had a weeding-iron. This was a length of iron stuck into a long handle. The business end of the iron was sharpened, and shaped into a V. So, armed with this simple but efficient tool, we proceeded to walk up and down the field, taking around a 5 ft span each, and stabbing the thistles that were popping up amongst the corn. The knack was to cut the main stem of the nasty intruder under the soil.

Very often, May can be cold, and as it was not a particularly energetic job, it could be far from pleasant, but we relied on the good old mark 1 hessian sacks, tied around our waists. Later I was to discover just how necessary this job was. No sooner was the corn-weeding behind us, the cabbages tilled, and the mangolds hoed, than hay-harvest burst upon us. The very words conjure up an idyllic picture of the sun shining, the sweet smelling hay piled high on the cart, and with several of the workers riding contentedly on the load. In fact, it was strenuous work over long hours, and a couple of days' rain could quickly ruin what had promised to be a good crop, adding extra labour, and ending up with inferior hay that the cows and young stock would not enjoy. The result would be less milk, and less weight-gain for the youngsters.

The grass was cut with the finger-type mower, pulled by the tractor on this farm. Then the horse was used to pull the machine that turned the crop. This would be employed several times if the crop was heavy, and the sunshine in short supply. When it was deemed fit to harvest, i.e., no moisture left in it, a horse-drawn rake would row-up the crop. A funny implement it was too. As it went along the curved tines collected the hay and the operator, who was perched on the seat tripped the rake at regular intervals, so that the crop was collected into neat rows all over the field. Most times, horses and carts then appeared, and we pitched the hay up on to the cart, using a two tine peak or pick. Once again, a knack was used, whereby one turned the peak over to unload it onto the cart. This made it easier to shed the bundle of hay, and also safer for the man on the cart, who, with a peak with a shorter handle or stick, placed the hay about and made the load.

At this farm, most of the hay was stored in Dutch barns, but if a rick was to be made in the field, preparations were necessary. A base for the hay was made with faggots of wood laid on the ground and sometimes topped by wads of straw which minimized waste. The hay was pitched off the load and one or two men, depending on the size of the rick, put the hay about and made the rick. At first it was fairly easy to unload the cart, as it would be downhill, but as the rick rose, so the job got harder, and so often one seemed to be standing on what one was striving to hoist up. The hay seeds and bits got into our hair, and fell down inside our shirts and stuck to our skin, we were perspiring so. Mr Lott also had a 'sweep', that cut out the need to pick it up from the field. Instead, this gadget, that resembled a huge comb, was fitted on the front of the tractor and the hay was collected by the sweep and taken to the rick site. There two men would pitch up the large pile of hay onto the rick, anxious to clear it before another sweepful arrived. When the sweepfuls came too quickly for the men to clear, the tractor driver would go to a more distant part of the field, to give the rick men a chance to catch up.

37

Sometimes the hay would be poked, usually if rain threatened before it was fit to carry. It was a time-consuming job, and labour-intensive, but doing so saved many a crop from being spoiled. Of course, during the war there were no weather forecasts, so the seasoned farmers were pretty good at judging the weather for themselves, by the wind, the clouds, and the sunsets. A lovely little flower called the scarlet pimpernel was also studied. It opened wide in bright conditions, and also opened in cloudy weather if no rain was about, but to find it closed was a sure sign of rain.

To get back to the pokes. They were large piles of hay, rather like outsize bee hives and care had to be taken to tidy up the outside of these to ensure minimal water damage if rain came. Really, to an onlooker, it presented an attractive picture, a hay field full of hay pokes. As usual, the reality was somewhat different, as, before the hay could be taken in, these pokes had to be spread out over the ground again to dry out, and later raked up prior to carrying.

If the weather was good, we worked till dark, and felt a deep sense of achievement and gratitude when the last lot was safely in. Any outside ricks had to be thatched, and this meant that rushes had to be mown and bundled up, and spars cut. These were sharpened wooden staples, made usually of hazel twigs and they secured the ropes that kept the rush thatching on the rick. Usually large stones were tied along the office, or eaves of the thatch as an extra precaution. To thatch a rick was a craft in itself, and I was only the dogsbody, and tended to the requirements of the thatcher.

Sometimes, if grass was plentiful, we made some silage as well. There was little science about it in those days as we carried it wet very often, and just piled it into a heap. Oddly enough, the cattle enjoyed it, but the wastage was high. Only the cows were fed with it; no one dreamed of giving silage to calves or sheep back in those days.

Actually, one other animal got an occasional fork-full, and that was the bull. He was a big red Shorthorn kept in a shed at the lower end of the yard. We fed and watered him through a large hole in the wall. I recall that lowering a bucket of water through the hole could be tricky, especially if the bull happened to be thirsty. He would thrust his huge head into the bucket before it reached the ground, and often force it out of ones' hands. After several incidents when I had to fish for the bucket with a pike, I hit on the idea of tying some binder-twine to the handle. I never dared to go into his shed as I was scared stiff of him, and not without reason. On one occasion he had chased one of the men round the muck-heap — scary!

CHAPTER THIRTEEN

HIGH SUMMER

There were sheep also on this farm, and sometimes I was sent out to count them, but never did much work with them, and now it was shearing time. In the barn was an engine which powered the mill, the circular saw, and the sheep clippers. Choosing a fine day, the sheep were brought in and shut in an enclosure which we had rigged up the previous day. My boss did the shearing, and I was soon instructed as to my job. I caught the sheep, dragged the reluctant beast to the shearing platform, then took away the fleece from the previous victim and tied it up. No cord was used but a length of wool was spun out and we used that as a tie. I can well remember, even now, my amazement as the beautiful clean wool was revealed. The sheep looked so drab on the outside, and it came as a real surprise to see the inner side of their coats. Any small nicks the sheep suffered were quickly treated with Stockholme tar to prevent fly-strike. My aim was to have the sheep ready for the boss when he wanted it, so not to hold up the good work. As the day wore on, the sheep seemed to get bigger and more obstinate and my hands, arms and clothes were by now very greasy and that didn't help. It must have been such a relief for those poor creatures, as they shot off back to the field, minus their thick coats.

The bundles of fleeces were stored in the barn until such time as the merchants came to collect them. They did tend to harbour mice, and the farm cats did a great job, keeping the vermin partly under control.

After the shearing was done, it was time to trim the hedges. A well-sharpened pruning hook, and a stick with a forked end were the tools required as Bert and I set off, he to show me, and I to learn the art of tidying up the hedges. The first lesson was always to get behind the brambles — much easier to cut that way. The stick was used to keep the prickly creepers away from one's arms and face, and to heap up the trimmings as one went along, making sure to cut out the bottom of the hedge, or one would face problems later, picking up the trimmings to be tipped away in an odd corner.

As it happened, I was not completely ignorant about this job. On my first farm, the boss handed me a hook, and took me to a hedge that looked like a drier version of the Amazon jungle, and said to pare it back. I set about the job with plenty of enthusiasm, but no skill, and seemed to be achieving nothing, except for scratched and bleeding hands and arms. Suddenly, an elderly man appeared, and said he would show me how to do it. "The secret is my dear," he said, "to get right in behind it," and he proceeded to demonstrate, telling me that he knew that particular hedge hadn't seen a hook for five years at least.

Periodically we stopped to sharpen our hooks. I never really got the hang of it and passed my hook over to Bert, who grumbled but always obliged. The roadside hedges we took particular pains with, as once again, they were open to inspection from all and sundry. The trimmings had to be picked up soon after cutting, or a man from the Council who rode around on a motor bike would remind you there were strict by-laws about this. When I see today's machines that pulverize everything in their path I marvel at their efficiency and speed. It used to take us weeks, I suppose, because then it was time to do the corn-field hedges as well.

The glorious fields of oats, and dredge corn, which was a mixture of oats and barley, were quickly changing colour, and the self-binder came out of hibernation for a good oil and grease, and close scrutiny to check for any obvious faults. But before the cutting could start, two jobs lay ahead; first to trim all the hedges, then to mow around. Because the binder would have crushed a fair area around the perimeter of the fields, we hand mowed these headlands using a scythe. I gazed in admiration as Bert or Bill swung this tool in steady rhythm and the corn fell before the sharpened blade. To sharpen a scythe was a more skilled job than a hook. I shuddered to myself as the stone was swept over the blade, expecting to see at worst a hand, at best a finger sliced off, but glad to say that never happened. My job was to follow and pick up the corn into sheaf size bundles and bind them, using the long lengths of stalks. One got the hang of it and eventually I could walk steadily behind the scythe man, bind the sheaf, drop it close to the hedge and never stop. Now the wisdom of trying to rid the field of thistles became obvious. Any that survived amongst the corn caused problems aplenty, as the prickles, though small, were painful, but fortunately Emily was good at fetching them out with a sharp needle and operated every evening on my hands.

Once the hedge swathe had been hand-mown, along came the binder behind the tractor, but I have seen a team of three horses pulling the binder, often a young lad would ride the front or fore horse. It was very hard work for the horses. The finger-type blade shuttled to and fro, then the cut corn fell onto a canvas base, that took the crop up to the trusser, where it was tied with cord and the finished sheaf shot out at the side. If the binder was correctly set, and the corn standing nicely, the sheaves would be tidy and easy to set, but if the crop was laid or the binder not right, the sheaves would be loustery — untidy and difficult to tell which was the ear or the butt end. After a few rounds, we proceeded 'to set the field up', in other words, to collect the sheaves and set them in groups of six all round the field, keeping to rows. When it was finished it looked great, the tighter together the stooks or shocks were, the heavier the crop.

Rabbits were plentiful and they tended to move away from the path of the binder, and into the standing crop. But, as their refuge became progressively reduced in size, they realized the time had come to make a run for safety, and they bolted out, in an attempt to make the shelter of the hedges. The dogs had a field day, chasing most of them, and catching quite a lot. And sometimes Bert would bring his twelve bore gun and bag a few. Rabbit was on the menu for a few days. They were roasted, put in a pie or stew, and baby ones were delicious fried. They provided a welcome boost to the meagre meat ration.

Mr Lott grew mostly oats or dredge-corn. Now barley has a spiky tail to each grain and these spikes seemed to have the ability to get everywhere, and they can be very irritating indeed. One year I recall wheat being grown. It was a winter variety, which meant it was planted in the autumn instead of the spring. When the ground began to warm up in March/April, the wheat shoots really took off, and to my amazement, the sheep were put into it, to eat off the tender shoots, and check its growth, and also to trample the ground and consolidate the plants. The big difference between wheat and other corn crops was that the shocks, or stooks contained 8 sheaves, as opposed to the usual six. The straw was much stiffer too, and unsuitable for use as bedding, and I think it was used for thatching.

CHAPTER FOURTEEN

CORN HARVEST

A brief respite followed, when the binder had finished its job. Depending on the weather, some 10 to 14 days were needed for the cut crop to ripen and harden up. We used this time to prepare the rick sites, cut and haul home rushes and generally prepare for the gathering in. If the weather was bad, very often the stooks had to be re-set, as the heavy heads of the sheaves, lying together, in prolonged wet conditions, could encourage the ears to sprout, and this impaired the quality of the crop. We moved from shock to shock, lifting and re-setting the sheaves on to fresh ground, and I have known times when this job had to be done twice, or even three times before the weather was right for it to be harvested. Sometimes before the binder moved into the field, strong winds, heavy rain, or persistent thick drizzle would make the standing crop bend over when the rooks would move in, causing yet more damage, both by devouring the grain, and also by further flattening the crop. To cut it presented a problem in that the cutter blade could ride over the laid corn and only a small quantity would find its way up over the canvas.

In an attempt to correct this, the binder would cut 'one way', that is only one or two sides of the crop, increasing the time it took to do the job, but at least salvaging more of the corn. When the sun shone, and the grain had hardened off, we went into the fields and pulled over the stooks, butt ends towards the breeze, to air them out.

Then along came the trailers and the hard work began, but it never seemed anything like as hard as haymaking. The drill was to pitch two sheaves at a time, the first couple of loads seemed light work, but by the end of the day, it was a different story. In a good summer, the straw would be a glorious golden colour, and rustle as one moved the sheaves, quite often one discovered tiny field mice nests under the shocks, or baby frogs would hop away to safety.

Only a moron could fail to enjoy the sights and sounds of nature that were free to us each day. Those golden days of autumn were somehow special, and it seemed as though the sun was never going to leave us, and I could understand Indian tribes worshipping the moon and wind and especially the sun which injects life into plants the world over.

Following the completion of the corn harvest, we prepared for winter. Bert and I would be sent out to do some fencing, but first we had to cut stakes for the job. There were some useful coppices down by the river, and armed with a hook and saw we cut down likely looking limbs, and sawed them into lengths. It was my job to nick off the smaller twigs and sharpen out the ends with an axe. Lots of hazel trees grew there, and the nuts drew me like a magnet! I used to crack them open on a large stone, using another stone as a hammer, and I recall Bert saying once to me, "Don't leave all those shells there in the track, the boss will notice them and know you have been wasting his time." Good advice, that I never after forgot!

Bert would dig a pit into which the stake was positioned, then I would hold it steady whilst he banged it in with an iron bar — or bar-ire, as it was called. It took a cool nerve to hold on to the post, and the heavy bar descended on its top. Bert assured me he never missed, or not very often anyway! Then the wire had to be nailed to the posts. In those days electric fences were unheard of, so it was barbed wire, the curse of many dairy cows who got entangled in it, causing dreadful damage to udders and teats. We usually suffered nasty tears in our hands and fingers too.

As we unrolled it, we tried to keep it taut, because the moment it slackened it twisted uncontrollably and the barbs bit into our clothes — at best — or our fingers at worst. Bert held the wire tightly against the post, and my job was to nail it in place. Bert urged me to hit it as hard as I could, telling me that the nail had no friends, so I could vent my anger — and strength upon it.

As the days shortened, and became colder, the young stock and milking cows were brought into the sheds, the former to stay there till next spring, but the cows went out by day to eat the kale thrown out for them and enable us to clean out the shippens to get ready for them to come back in. Once more we all settled back into a winter regime. In those days I cannot remember that I dreaded the approach of winter as I do now. I expect the young blood coursed faster through my body then!

CHAPTER FIFTEEN

STRANGE FOLK AND CURES

As in all communities, we had our share of odd characters. One I particularly remember was called Bill Bromell. He lived in a small cottage called Pleddymede, quite close to where I lived. I think his mother lived there too, certainly it wasn't his wife as he never married. He was a funny little man, of small build, not over blessed with brain power but in many ways very sharp. He rode a bicycle, and was a special policeman during those war years, and he often stopped outside our house to tell us proudly he was off on Point duty. What he would have done if confronted by a German parachutist, I cannot guess!

But although his mental ability was not the greatest, he had other talents. He could charm away warts and ringworms, both in humans and animals, and he also was able, on one occasion, to perform a near miracle. A neighbour was trimming a hedge with the only tool available for the job, i.e., a bill-hook, when the hook slipped on some rotten vegetation, and severed the artery in his wrist. Now at that time, this would have been serious indeed. Nobody had any first aid knowledge, so by the time the doctor had arrived from Bradworthy, the patient could well have been dead. But help was at hand in the shape of Billy Bromell. Seeing the gravity of the situation, with blood spurting freely from the victim's wrist, Billy dashed into a nearby cattle shed where he seized a handful of cobwebs that were festooned around the walls, rushed back to the patient and proceeded to staunch the flow of blood with the cobwebs.

Believe it or not, it worked, and when the doctor eventually arrived, he could not believe what he saw. The only one who was not surprised was Billy who probably could not understand what the fuss was about and calmly went about his business, leaving the doctor to tidy up the wound. Now I had been brought up with a firm belief that there was no such thing as witchcraft or magic, so the matter-of-fact way that folk talked of having warts put away by a local magician quite frankly appalled and at the same time frightened me.

Imagine my horror when Emily calmly said that Billy was going to call by to charm away some warts on young Kenny's hands! I could not make her to reconsider it, Billy had already treated some yearlings with ringworm with complete success, but the thought of the fair-haired little lad being subjected to some weird rites or incantations, made me shudder. Billy duly called by and I was ready to bolt to my room, but he dealt with the child on his own, and was gone before you could say abracadabra! Later I got Kenny on his own and asked what had happened. Ken said he muttered things he could not understand, but never touched him. I expect you have guessed that within a few weeks the offending warts had disappeared.

I remember discussing this with Mr Lott soon afterwards and asking him if he felt this strange power was from God or the devil. He said he did not know, but for his part, preferred not to take any risks by dabbling with it — a sentiment I fully shared. I was given a quick cure on one occasion, but not by a charmer. I had a really heavy cold, and was under the weather. Bill assured me he had just the remedy, and fetched in a bottle of dark brown liquid from the stable window. When the dust and cobwebs were cleared away, it was possible to read the label "Revivium" quick remedy for horses with the cough. Bill assured me he had taken it with good results, so I swallowed some of the evil-looking potion and felt that someone had lit a flaming torch in my chest. I was on fire! Bill, Emily and the boys were laughing their socks off. I could only stagger up the stairs to bed, perspiring like a steeplechaser. As far as I recall, the cold and cough succumbed to the fiery potion, and departed. My amazement lay in the fact that I had survived it!

Next door to us was another smallholder, with much the same mishmash of stock and arable land. To help augment his income, he became the local 'vet', and would travel around on his bicycle with the tools of his trade strapped to the crossbar of the bike, and various medicines and ointments carried in a knapsack on his back. It goes without saying that he had never received any real instruction or training for the jobs he undertook, but I suppose he had learned by experience and that can be a pretty tough, but usually effective school. So it was that any farmer with a sick beast would summon the 'vet', and off he would go to try out his skill on the said animal. I don't think he could have had many real disasters, as he was in constant demand. Oh yes, there were vets available, but were avoided if at all possible, partly because of the fear of a hefty bill, and also I guess, because this chappie was all part of the community and was trusted. And of course, he brought snippets of gossip to mull over, along with the pills and bottles of cure-alls!

CHAPTER SIXTEEN

NEW IDEAS

Mr Lott was clearly a man born 30 years too soon. Today, organic farming is very much in vogue, but in the forties very few people had ever heard of it and of those, even fewer could have explained the theory behind it. But Mr Lott had read a book, written by an eminent scientist, and was very impressed by what he had read and determined to put some of its ideas into practice. The author of this book had explained how over-cultivation of the land in North America had contributed to the dust bowls there, where top soil, so lacking in humus had blown away, leaving bowls or pans of completely useless dusty earth in which no crops could flourish.

The prediction was that we could witness similar situations in this country if farmers kept taking out of the land and not putting back. Of course, fertilizers, though in short supply, were being spread over the land, but that life-giving constituent, humus, which is a product of rotting plant and animal material, was being depleted. It was in stunned silence that Bert and Bill were informed that there was to be no further fertilizer used on the land, but instead we would make compost — another new word for us. The boss explained that this was really rotted vegetable material and that, to get it going, we would collect all hedge trimmings, waste material such as silage waste, rick waste, chaff after a threshing and anything to create a compost heap. If it was properly made, it should heat up a destroy all harmful seeds from nettles, docks and the like, and also it would encourage earthworms. After this shattering news had sunk in a bit, Bert pronounced it a complete waste of time, but Bill, who had taken orders since he could talk — and still did — from his shrew-like wife, merely grunted and quoted his favourite maxim, "The one who pays has the say".

In our small community news of this about-turn farming practice soon spread round, and of course I got questioned a lot, as I was supposed to know. Actually I had gleaned a bit more information, as Mr Lott, perhaps sensing a sympathetic ear, explained the organic principle to me at some length, and I was beginning to see that maybe — just maybe — this idea held water. But I had not at that time had the job of turning over the heap, i.e., forking it all over, working right down to ground level. What made it so difficult was that brambles and some small twigs and branches that had gone in with the hedge trimmings, were exactly the same as the day they had been put there, so it was hard work trying to tug them out and turn them over.

But there was worse to come Mr Lott decided that, in order to get a supply in hand for the following year, we would also pick up our near neighbours' trimming for them and haul them back to our compost heaps. Can you imagine the jokes and jibes that were levelled at this? In the evenings such remarks as, "Don't bother about your hedge-trimming, Farmer Lott will send his Land Girl to pick them up," or, "Bet Farmer Lott will have a bumper crop of docks and nettles next year. Will he harvest that?" I could go on. Now I really admired Mr Lott and thought he could do no wrong, plus the fact that I was fiercely loyal, so it was that these remarks hurt deeply, partly, I suspect, because I felt that the compost heaps were less than perfect and the doubt factor was beginning to creep in.

When the stuff was spread the following spring, we had orders to pitch the large brambles to one side. I believe the boss waited for a good day and put a match to them. That year the weather was glorious, so the crops looked good, whether because of the compost, or the residue of artificial fertilizer, I don't know. Meanwhile, Mr Lott had read another book, which resulted in our haymaking becoming a thing of wonder for this area. In Scotland, where the seasons are pretty fickle, crops, both hay and corn, are slung over tripods to dry out and it is claimed, to prevent deterioration in bad conditions!

Now where he got those tripods from I never asked, but they arrived in late May, just in time for hay harvest. We viewed them with intense suspicion. We had never seen anything like it, and the only thing they reminded me of was Indian wigwams that I'd seen in a Western film at the cinema!.

They consisted of three long poles, joined at one end and a plentiful supply of triangular shaped wires, of two different sizes. A few days after the grass had been cut, we loaded up these weird contraptions and hauled them to the field. Then under the boss's direction, we proceeded to erect them. They were spread out with the larger wire dropped over the top, holding it in shape, then the smaller wire was also passed over the top, so that we finished up with a tripod of three poles, over which were draped two wire bands.

It would hardly be described as a high tech job, and we soon had the 'wigwams' erected. But ah! then came the hard work, as we gathered together the half made hay and attempted to drape it over the wires. Try as I would, my pike-fulls just seemed to slither to the ground, usually *inside* the wires. A quick glance at the other chaps, and I could see they were not any more adept at it than I and their muttered curses confirmed that. But by trial and error, and in my case, use of my hands, we got a bit better at it and eventually the whole crop in that largish field was hung over these wires. Meanwhile I debated which would be the best course of action that evening. No way could it go unnoticed by the neighbours that was certain. After all, they stood about 6 ft high!

So, should I go home and casually mention the new system, or sit tight and wait for the inevitable storm to break. I need not have worried myself. When I got back in the evening, I was greeted with a barrage of questions so it took a while to explain what they were. The general consensus of opinion was that these newfangled things just might be OK in Scotland, but here in the west country, good old pokes beat the tripods by a long chalk — and I could not summon the energy to argue. The weather was wonderful, so that, as it turned out, neither tripods or pokes were needed, and we had the task of off loading the grass/hay from the wires, which was almost as tedious as putting it on had been. Quite a few of the tripods got pulled over as we tried to get our peaks into the grass, some smart foot work was called for to avoid getting a nasty wallop and a few poles got broken. Then the tripods had to be collected together before we could start to collect the crop. I believe we dumped them against the hedge pro tem, as they were to be used for the corn crop too.

We did find that getting the sheaves on to the tripods was much easier, probably because we did it by hand then finished off the top with a sheaf turned 'inside out ' so that the ears rested on the top, and the straw spread out around looked quite effective. The glorious weather just went on and on, and the large jug of home-made lemonade placed in the shade drew us like a magnet. At last the corn was fit to be carried in, and once again, we had to get the sheaves off the tripod wires, and move the tripods away from the path of the horses and tractor. Then the corn was safely tucked away in ricks, or in the Dutch barn.

Mr Lott told me one morning to harness the mare Bess, into the cart, then go out into the fields to collect the tripods, so that they could be stored away for the winter. He suggested that I hung the triangular wires over the front lade, and put the wooden poles into the cart. Now on the face of it, that seemed a perfectly simple and reasonably easy task — or so I thought. But I had not reckoned on Bess's flighty habits, although I had already had experience of her moods.

For a time, all went well, the poles gradually piled up on the cart, and the wires hung safely from the lade. As we passed through a rough gateway, the wires began to rattle against each other and create a right old jangle. That was enough — nay, too much for the nervous beast, and she set off across the field, at first quite slowly, but as the wires began to bounce about, her pace quickened and she went into a canter. No way could I match her speed. I could only watch in dismay as the wires shot off the lade, and the poles bounced out of the cart.

To reach the yard two gateways had to be navigated, one from the field into the lane, and another through the wide opening into the yard. There wasn't much point in running, but I hurried off in pursuit, listening out for the sound of smashing timber that would realize my worst fears, namely that Bess and cart were in a crumpled heap ahead.

I could scarcely believe my eyes when I saw Bess and cart, both intact at the bottom of the yard, outside the stable. Mr Lott must have witnessed the sudden, swift arrival of the horse and cart, rushed out to find out what had happened, discovered I was not there, and feared the worst. He was very relieved to see me all in one piece. I thought he looked very pale! As for the offending tripods, they were distributed over a wide area, and had to be retrieved later, with the steadier Henry.

CHAPTER SEVENTEEN

ALL IN A DAY'S WORK

Having already mentioned that I had had a few adventures with Bess, I will now try to recall exactly what happened. On one occasion, the boss had gone over to Parkham to a farm sale and had bought a butt there. So the next day he told me to ride the mare over to Parkham, put her into the shafts and bring back the purchase to the farm. Bert suddenly remembered that his brother-in-law, who lived in Parkham village, had promised him some seed potatoes, so could I stop by to collect them. This all seemed perfectly straightforward, so off I set, relishing the view of the fields from the mare's back, and enjoying the ride.

Someone helped me get Bess tackled up into the butt, so all I had to do now, was to stop at a cottage to collect the seed potatoes. The journey over to Parkham hadn't sapped the energy of the mare, and I sensed there would be problems if I left her unattended whilst I collected the potatoes, but luck was with me. A lad appeared on a bicycle, and I asked if he would be kind enough to hold on to the horse's head, whilst I called at the cottage. I was given a box of superb seed potatoes, with lovely dark green shoots (chits). I placed them carefully in the bottom of the butt, climbed on board, thanked the helpful boy and headed for home.

Bess knew we were on the return trip, so before long she broke into a gentle trot, which progressed rapidly into a canter. No amount of tugging on the reins or shouting whoa! had any effect. I can only feel grateful, as I look back, that we met no cars or other road users. After a mile or so, she slackened down, and then it was I was able to take my eyes off the road to glance at the potatoes. Horror of horrors! They had all been bounced out of the box and rolled madly around in the bottom of the butt, like the lottery balls. The chits lay in the bottom too, they had parted company from the potatoes long since. I pulled the horse to a halt, and with one hand firmly grasping the reins, I retrieved the seeds, replaced them in the box, collected the limp, bruised shoots and pitched them over the side. I felt the worst was over, but there was more to come. I turned into the narrow lane at Cranford, which leads directly to Lone Barton. In places it is quite narrow, and as yet, no hedge trimming had been done. Some of the overgrown brambles brushed against the mare's back and flanks, and with a snort of rage, she took off again. I calculated that no way could we overturn, the lane was too narrow for that, so again, I just held grimly on and let her go. We negotiated the sharp right-hand bend and as we approached the yard gate, she slowed up, tired out I expect.

As Bert had now gone home to dinner, I merely collected the potatoes together again, put the box in the shed, whilst I parked the butt, and tied Bess up in the stable. When Bert saw the seed potatoes, he grumbled a bit, saying that Reuben had promised him well-chitted tubers, and these had none. I merely looked innocent — I think — and murmured my commiserations!

The other occasion when Bess bolted, was potentially more dangerous. I was sent out to turn a field of hay, the turner was a contraption with rotating tines, mounted on wooden bars with the uncomfortable iron seat perched on one side. It was a hot day, the hay smelt delicious, but the flies were biting. I think Bess must have been bitten because — yes! you've guessed — she bolted!

Again, it was quite impossible to slow her up, or even control where she was going. My concerns were to try to stay on board, and to steer her away from the hedge in good time. Never was hay tossed so high into the air, as we dashed madly on. Out of the corner of my eye I spotted the boss who had come out to see how the hay was coming along. I think he took in the whole situation at a glance. He came as near as he dared and yelled to me to let her have her head and concentrate on staying atop the crazy implement. Of course, she slowed down eventually, but we had made a right mess of the rows of hay, which were now scattered widespread over the field.

I pulled the horse to a halt, and once again my boss looked very concerned and said he would finish the field, and I could go in and find a few odd jobs to do before dinner time. Looking back at these incidents now, I realize just how much at risk I was, but at the time, I thought it all good stuff — a bit funny in fact. Call it the foolhardiness of youth!

CHAPTER EIGHTEEN

BUYING AND SELLING

Up in the village of Woolsery, there was an auction field, where every month, farmers brought animals to be sold by the local auctioneer, a Mr Cory. The village pub stayed open all day, and hot lunches were served to visiting dealers, and the auctioneer and his staff, whilst many of the farmers gathered there too for a pint or two and a lively discussion about the current market trends and prices. Store cattle, sheep and barren cows were usually taken back to the farm, even if sold, until the buyer could arrange drovers to collect them.

Sometimes it was a couple of weeks before they finally left the vendor's farm. Dairy cows were nearly always sold with their new-born calf, in fact it was regarded as suspicious if there was no calf. Could it be that the cow had had a dead calf, or had she been calved for several weeks. The cow that was to be sold was milked fairly late the evening before the market, and not milked at all on market day morning, so of course her udder would be pretty full by the time she entered the ring. Her calf would be muzzled so that it could not steal a feed from its mother, but it would have been either fed by hand in the morning, or allowed to suckle another cow. The prospective buyers would look at the horns to try to determine her age, as each year produced another ring on the horns. The skin would be pinched up, her mouth peered into, but most important, her udder would be studied from all angles, and felt with searching fingers to discover if there were any lumps. The vendor would usually strip out some milk to prove that she was quiet — a nervous kick could instantly knock a pound or so off the price — remember that most cows were still hand milked. Of course, the dealers vied with each other to secure a purchase. Often, if a farmer fancied a cow, or indeed any animals at the market, it paid him to keep quiet and let the dealers get on with it and approach the successful dealer after the animal had been knocked down and buy it from him. Obviously money was involved, but it still probably worked out cheaper than trying to out-bid the dealers. Now my boss, unlike many local farmers, did not go to market much unless he had stock to sell, or needed to buy some. A lot of farmers looked on it as a day out, a sort of social occasion when they met their neighbours to exchange news and views.

So it came as a bit of a surprise when the boss announced he was planning to sell a freshly calved heifer and her calf the following day and he wanted me to go with him to drive the beast around the ring. I was secretly well pleased, but nervous as a kitten, as I was still very shy and wondered what sort of reception I would get. The heifer was a sweet creature, and I duly prodded her around the ring and proved her docile nature by squeezing jets of milk from the swollen udder. All was going nicely and the bids were mounting up, when one big dealer, with a red face, suggested in a loud voice that the land girl be included in the deal. My face flushed at the laughter that followed, and I wished myself back scraping up the yard, but fortunately the heifer was knocked down and I was saved further embarrassment!

Before I leave the subject of the local market, one further point of interest. The freshly calved cows had to be partly milked out after sale, to relieve both their udders and general discomfort. Local women would oblige, and they were allowed to have the milk. Bert's wife used to do this, and she, being a thrifty soul, would scald the milk to make butter, a scarce luxury in those war-time days! She also made wonderful rice puddings with the buttermilk. I believe someone who lived up at Cranford also milked out cows. The mind boggles at the thought of carrying a heavy pail of milk that far, with a steep hill to face!

Many farmers' wives had separators, a complex but most efficient machine designed to take the cream out of the milk, which was cooked over a steamer, until a delicious thick crust formed, then cooled on the blue-slate slabs in the farm dairy. The machine was turned by hand, and not until the correct speed had been reached, sometimes indicated by the silencing of a bell, was the milk allowed to flow out of the top 'receiver' or round bowl, and over a revolving set of cups; soon 'skimmed' or separated milk shot out of the milk spout, positioned over a bucket, then more slowly, the cream trickled out of the cream spout into an enamelled bowl.

On one occasion, Mrs Lott had used the separator, scalded the cream and asked me if I would take it down to the well. As I recall, it was thundery weather and she reckoned that it would be cooler resting on the water in the well, than in the dairy. The well wasn't too far away, in a small field or 'plat' at the bottom of the yard. I duly obliged, then went about my work. That afternoon, I was again needed to go to the well, to bring the bowl of cream back to the house. Mrs Lott had been busy cooking, as the next day a thresh was planned so needed the cream for the traditional apple-pie.

When I stooped down to lift out the cream I was surprised to see a half-grown frog sitting happily on its golden crust, and as I set the bowl down the frog blinked at me in the sudden sunlight. I lifted the frog off and started back, but *en route* I decided to keep quiet about it, as I knew Mrs Lott would have had a difficult struggle with her conscience had I told her. I took the view that 'ignorance is bliss' and heartily tucked into my share of the cream the next day. I never heard that any of us suffered any ill effects!

CHAPTER NINETEEN

WINTER'S WORST

And so the years slipped by. I was regarded as a member of the family at my lodgings over at Alminstone Cross, and almost one of the family too, at Lane Barton. By this time, I knew most of the local folk, and had it not been for the war, I guess I was happy. The two Lott boys, Gordon and Eric, came home for their holidays from boarding school, and the two girls, Christine and Connie were soon to go to the village school.

When the boys were home, they had to help around the farm, and Gordon couldn't wait to get his hands on the tractor, or yet the car, given half a chance! Both took turns to help me milk, but neither was particularly keen on this as they much preferred going out with their air-gun trying to get magpies or starlings.

I remember asking Eric to wash off a cow — in those days an udder bucket and cloth were the obvious signs of good hygiene! Tending to another cow, I thought I heard a slight thud and turning round saw Eric in a heap by the wall. His nervous, arms' length approach had frightened the normally quiet beast so she had reacted in the way that cows have, by kicking out at him. He was completely winded and rather frightened, so I took him in and believe that just about marked the end of his milking experience.

But Gordon, after making allowances for the odd bout of careless high spirits, only natural in a teen-age lad, was fast becoming an asset, and we got along well together and enjoyed quite a lot of banter and practical jokes.

One morning, we were sent out with halters to fetch in the two horses, the flighty Bess and the more reliable Henry. Now, on my own, I would have caught the horses and walked in with them. But that idea did not please Gordon who decided he was going to ride Bess, and I was going to ride Henry. He gave me a leg up, pulled Bess to the side of the hedge, from where he performed a flying leap on to her back. So far, so good, then, without warning, he slapped Henry's rear end sharply, at the same time digging his heels into the mare's flanks. "Race you!" he yelled, as we galloped full tilt along the field. Now I was passably good at staying on board a horse, if it was equipped with a saddle and reins, but with neither of these vital requirements, not as easy by a long chalk. I was quite content to be the loser of the race, what I wasn't happy about was the prospect of hitting the deck like a heavy sack of spuds. It was a case of survival tactics, I clung tighter to the horse's mane than Sinbad the Sailer clung to his bearers and praise be, I reached the yard safely, a close second I might add. As usual, my early fear had been exchanged for excited exhilaration, so the ticking-off the grinning lad ought to have had, never materialized.

Meanwhile, I was beginning to see the writing on the wall. It was clear that Gordon was going to come home to work as soon as he left school, and I could see that there would not be sufficient work for all of us. However I pushed the thought to the back of my mind and decided to wait and see how it all worked out. The year was 1947, and the New Year had brought some very cold weather and flurries of snow, but it wasn't until the 29th of the month that the blizzard struck.

I had never seen snow like it, and when we looked up the air was full of flakes and very quickly the landscape became a winter wonderland. Back home, they had been busy giving the potatoes an extra covering of straw, and getting in hay from outside ricks for cattle use. The boys and I kept peeping out of the door, to get an up-to-date picture of the weather, and each time we did so, the snow was that much deeper. We huddled round the open fire and wondered what tomorrow would bring. The next day, the snow lay deep, and there was no question of using my bike to go to work. I trudged through the snow to find, on my arrival, that the boss had shovelled away a path from the back door to the milking sheds, and was already on the job. It was difficult to describe the events that followed, the hard work, the disruption and the suffering both to man and beast. I do remember that the cows were unable to go out at all, and gradually they got smellier and smellier, in spite of our best efforts to keep them, and the sheds, clean. Mrs Lott had a few fowls, who were quite puzzled by the strange, cold, white carpet, and in the end, they too had to be confined indoors, as their legs had become raw from plunging through the snow.

We fed the cows as best we could, but no kale or green stuff could be got at, so big inroads were made on the hay and straw ricks. Nearly every morning, it seemed there had been further over-night snowfall, as yesterday's tracks would be gone. The temperatures were low, but that did not cause as much havoc as in

1963, as there was not much plumbing — most folk relying on the trusty pump for water.

My bedding was reinforced by Bills Home Guard greatcoat, and my life-line, at night, was a hot-water bottle my sister gave me. It seemed it would go on for ever, and everyone soon found out that the early thrill at seeing the near-Arctic landscape, soon palled, and we began to get heartily sick of it. At the farm, there was nothing we could do except feed the stock, clean them out and milk the cows. Mr Lott left us to it and took up a hobby that was to be an outlet for a remarkable talent dormant till then.

He started painting pictures, to me they looked splendid from the word go, but I know that over the years his artistic skill improved so much and he exhibited paintings which were much admired. So, for him, at least, it opened a door. One weekend, after a particularly heavy fall of snow, Mrs Lott suggested that I might like to sleep at the farm, to save the energy sapping trudge to and fro work, also I would be on the spot, so to speak. I don't think Emily was too well pleased, but I accepted with alacrity, and slept in a small room that overlooked the higher yard. What I do remember especially, was the nightly ritual of warming the beds, using an old-fashioned copper warming-pan, which usually hung, highly burnished, in the hall. It had a long wooden handle and hot coals from the fire were shovelled into the circular bowl, the lid firmly clamped down, and Mrs Lott would carry it upstairs, to pass the hot pan up and down between the sheets. We all jumped into bed soon after, before the sheets had time to cool. Needless to say central heating was unheard of anywhere, and the rooms were like ice-boxes. Many times I've seen the fern-like traceries of ice *inside* the window, where our breath had frozen. Our clothes, left in a pile on the floor, were pretty chilly too, so we didn't linger around, and dragged our clothes on and dashed down the stairs to the comparative warmth of the kitchen! Good thing that we largely ignored make-up, the idea of shivering before a mirror and trying to apply mascara or lipstick in sub-zero temperature doesn't bear thinking about.

At the end of a week, the snowfall had been light, and there were tracks on the road where various horse drawn and motorized vehicles had passed, so I decided to return home. They were all so pleased to have me back, I felt a twinge of guilt at having left them, but this was somewhat eased when John confided to me that they had all shared the blankets from my bed and who could blame them!

56

One Sunday afternoon, part-way through this trying time, I was going back to the farm to milk, as Mr Lott had to go off to a nearby chapel to preach. I had also agreed to see the sheep before milking. As it was a grand, sunny day, I decided to call on a very dear friend first, then make my way over the fields to the farm, counting and checking on the sheep *en route*.

Dear old Grannie Arnold was another of this world's saints, and I loved her dearly. A mug of hot tea and a thick slice of bread, syrup and cream fortified me for the cross-country trip. I merely stepped over the gates, just the top bar visible above the driven snow. The sheep were in the middle of the field, where the snow had been blown off and they somehow managed to find a bit of herbage, but this was supplemented with hay. The whole world, it seemed to me, was a winter wonderland, and although the snow made hard work of even the simplest task, I had little to grumble about. I was warm, well-fed and had a job — many were worse off. So, we dragged through the whole of February and into the latter part of March. As soon as we began to think it would soon end, another fall of snow would set us right back again.

But whilst there was still plenty of snow around, I was to experiment with a possible cure for my chilblains. These had been a real misery for me every winter, and I guess warming one's feet before the open fire did not help, but I suffered so badly from cold feet. Anyway, Bill told me that if I ran barefoot through the snow, that would cure my chilblains for all time. Watched by the boys and Emily, I took a deep breath, and boldly dashed out into the white wilderness. Alas! this exercise did not do the trick, but at least the onlookers had a bit of entertainment, and I had a round of applause. Another cure had been already suggested, and involved dipping one's feet into the contents of the chamber-pot — that I could not face!

At last, we could detect a slight kindness in the air, as the wind swung round to a warmer direction. Remember, there were no weather forecasts right through the war, and we had to predict the weather ourselves as best we could. We told ourselves that there would soon be a thaw and wonder what we would find under that blanket of snow. The grand finale was yet to come.

I had been using the horse in the butt that morning probably to move around some hay or other fodder, when it began to rain and I told myself that the end was in sight. It was time to go to dinner so I took the horse down outside the stable. I was a bit surprised when his foot slipped on the ground, but it was only when I came to take off his harness that I discovered that every bit that was exposed to the wet, now had a thin casing of ice, and tiny beads of ice hung from his mane. The yard itself was like a skid-pan, not helped by the fact it was on the slope anyhow. I jumped on my bike — how stupid can you be? But as I attempted to negotiate the sharp left hand bend at the bottom of the hill, my bike and I parted company and I slid along the ground like a self-propelled toboggan! I gingerly picked myself up and pushed my bike into a gateway, there being little fear of theft in those days, and carefully walked home. The phone wires and every twig and leaf were hanging with ice, and suddenly it was a crystallized world — another wonderful sight — but potentially more dangerous than the snow had been. We slipped and slithered along, and I remember Bert coming to work with old socks over his boots. However, that was winter's final spiteful fling, and gradually the snow went away. Amazingly, underneath, the grass was green and the bare parts of a field, in the middle, were brown and lifeless by comparison. It took a long time to go away, which was probably to the good, had it all melted at once, we would have been flooded.

CHAPTER TWENTY

ALL CHANGE

It was the summer of 1947, I was now 21, and Reg and I had begun to search in earnest for the tenancy of a small farm that would get us started in farming. Each time we had a go, and tendered for a holding, our spirits rose and we awaited the outcome with suppressed excitement. But as the list of failures grew, so, too, did my despondency, but fortunately I enjoyed my work, so that eased my depression, and helped put it behind me. Gordon was to leave school soon, Bert had found work with the Forestry Commission, and the other land girl had also departed and Bill had been gone for some time. I was prepared for being told I was surplus to requirements but what I was totally unprepared for was when Mr Lott told me he was going to sell the cows and go into beef.

Perhaps it was a good thing in a way, as by this time I was so involved with the cows, and their management, that even at home,

I don't think I would have been really happy without them. And so, the local community gathered and the auctioneer sold off the cows to the highest bidder. I was kept busy, helping drive the cows round the makeshift ring, and answering lots of queries about yield, temperament, and age of animals. If I felt sad then, little did I even guess that in about 30 years time, I would see my own beloved cows pass to others and the almost inconsolable pain I would feel. There was still plenty to do, sheep to shear, harvesting to attend to, so I stayed on till the September. The authorities found me another job, this time not in the area, but near Bideford. So it was a case of change all round, not only to a new job, but I had to bid a sad farewell to the Harding family, promising to come back to see them soon. Also, it would not be easy for Reg and I to meet, we only had two nights out together as it was, but this would really restrict us.

My few belongings, plus bicycle, were loaded up and off I went. Weach Barton is situated about 2 miles from Bideford, on the old Barnstaple road, it had quite a long, tree lined avenue to reach it. A large house, with pleasant lawns, it stood at the end of a yard, with a range of buildings beyond.

I must admit I didn't really take to my new employers, yes, I had been spoiled I know, and would find it difficult indeed to find people like Mr and Mrs Lott, or the Harding family. But I decided that maybe I'd get used to it all, given time, but alas I was soon to discover that what they needed was a domestic servant, not a Land Girl at all. About the only outside job I did was to milk by hand the 10/12 cows. It wasn't that hand milking upset me, I liked it, and soon felt at home with the cows. But the rest of the time, the lady of the house kept me hard at it indoors, polishing furniture, dusting, sweeping carpets and cleaning silver. I could go on and on, but for the first time since becoming a Land Girl, I was unhappy; until then, a feeling I had not known.

Almost at once, I began to plan how I could leave without giving the impression that I was over hasty in throwing in the towel. At this farm, they reared a lot of turkeys for the Christmas trade, and I could not find it in my heart to leave them high and dry, when they were going to be so busy, so I determined to stay the course until the New Year. Anyone who has ever had any experience of turkeys, will know what delicate, temperamental creatures they are. The stupid birds would never voluntarily enter their night quarters, and it was a tricky problem to judge the right time to start rounding them up.

Go too soon, and they were absolutely uncontrollable, rushing here, there and everywhere, so it was impossible to do anything with them. Leave it too late, and they would have disappeared, preferring the trees to their cosy roost. What a job to get them down, but if left there, the local foxes would have had a pre-Christmas feast. So it was a case of climbing up a ladder to push the gormless creatures to the ground. When we got the timing just right, we had long runner bean sticks to help round them up so there was a huge sigh of relief all round when we could unhook the cover of the pop-hole to secure them for the night. My employer's wife sat in the market on Tuesdays and Saturdays so on Mondays and Fridays we plucked chickens and old hens for the stall. Now this was not a new job for me as I had done this for Mrs Lott oft-times, but Mrs Lott had always been most particular about the quality of the birds; any suspicious swellings and the bird would be discarded, but I found that at Weach Barton, anything would do, lumps were cut out and other blemishes camouflaged. I was horrified, but learnt to keep quiet. My opinion of my employers consequently dropped and I felt I'd be far happier out of it.

At this point I must relate a rather strange story. In the house there was, of course, no mains power supply, but there was a generator which provided lights for the house. There was no storage for the power, so, when the generator was turned off, that was it, one used the mark 1 candles. One evening, I had been to the pictures in Bideford, and on my return, my employers were in bed and the generator switched off. My candle and a box of matches were conveniently placed on the end of the kitchen table, so I lit it, and went to bed. Now my bedroom was at the far end of the house, and one went down a step to enter it. It was a rough, gusty November night, and the trees had swayed and moaned as I pushed my bike up that long drive. And now the candle spluttered and cast weird shadows on the walls, but it would have taken more than that to frighten me at that time.

But as I stepped down into my room, I was immediately struck by the intense chill in the atmosphere; which I then dismissed as a touch of winter. There was a small mirror on the wall at the bottom of my bed and I glanced idly in it, to comb back my hair. To my great surprise, someone was looking over my left shoulder, and was reflected plainly in the mirror. I spun round to confront the stranger, only to find I was quite alone in my room. I can honestly say I can't remember even feeling particularly frightened, startled yes, but certainly not in terror. I leapt into bed, pulled the covers over my head and slept like a baby. The next day I decided to keep quiet about it and almost convinced myself it was a trick of the fluttering candlelight.

Over thirty years later I heard that the house was reputed to be haunted, now at the time I was completely ignorant of that and in a funny way, I felt more fear when I heard of it than I did when it happened.

Well, time dragged by, each week seemed like a month, but in early December I wrote to the Land Army supervisor, asking her to move me again, preferably closer to Woolsery, telling her of my many domestic duties, and how little I was required outside. And I also screwed up all my courage and told my employers I would be leaving in early January. They did their best to dissuade me, but I was not to be influenced. When they saw that I was determined to go, they accused me of wanting to get back closer to my fiancé. There was an element of truth in that, but I would have put up with that if I had been happy, working outside and busy all day. Although I could have left immediately, I told them I would stay over to help get the turkeys done.

So about a week before Christmas we started, the boss did the killing and pulled out the quill feathers, then passed the birds over to me and a man, who was slightly simple minded, and also worked there. The clean picked birds were then taken indoors to the kitchen, where the farmer's wife dressed them for the oven. I almost enjoyed it, somehow the place *looked* more like a farm house kitchen, with a few feathers drifting around, and large paper sacks to hold the entrails. We grabbed a snack lunch, no knives and forks or saucers, and it all seemed far more down-to-earth.

The birds for slaughter were selected very quietly so as not to alarm the other excitable creatures, those whose lives were to be spared another few days were let out as usual. Those on the death list were confined in a smaller house. The "boss" collected them, two by two, for the chop.

I heard a bit of a commotion when he entered the death chamber, most men would have been swearing, but he was just muttering, I suppose it could have been swearing, but I don't think so!

We dropped our half naked birds and dashed in to see what the problem was. I suppose the frequent visits, and the gradual decline in numbers had somehow brought out the evil nature of one cock bird who had attacked two of his companions. One was dead, the other nearly, so the boss hastily strung them up and slit their throats in the hope they would bleed properly. But that was not the main problem, the spurs of the aggressive cock bird had torn into his two victims so there was no way of covering up their injuries with a layer of fat. Turkeys can take fright at their own shadow, and I've hated them ever since: except when they are well cooked!

Now this is where the farmer's wife's skill manifested itself. We plucked these two birds, took them to her, when she cut away all the torn bits, and with superb artistry and knowledge of the bone structure of a bird, she lashed them together with metal skewers and string, and just about made one good one out of the two, which they ate for Christmas dinner. Fortunately I dined elsewhere.

So, for about five or six days we were at it, and by the time they were all done, our thumbs and fingers were extremely tender. I have to admit, they looked good, all ranged along the blue slate slabs in the dairy, covered with milky white fat and decorated with sprigs of parsley. It was certainly an experience.

Meanwhile I had received word that I was to move to Ford Farm in Hartland, so I packed my bags, metaphorically shook the dust off my boots, and left Weach Barton, never to return.

CHAPTER TWENTY-ONE

MILK ROUND

The differences between Ford Farm and Weach Barton were great. There was a proper farm house, with three lively youngsters, a large open fireplace in the back kitchen and a black iron range in the living room, with a huge well scrubbed kitchen table and a long form on which the young ones sat. An Aga cooker took pride of place and was the focal point of the room — funny how anyone who came in went straight to it and stood with their back towards its warmth.

A limited supply of hot water was obtained from a tap at the bottom, and of course this water, held in a boiler at the back, had to be topped up, in other words, what one took out had to be replaced. In the back kitchen was the open chimney which was kept alight most of the time, and the wet coats and boots were dried there overnight.

I found my new boss a very easygoing type so I soon settled into my new home and job. The milking chore was soon left to me, I liked it that way, but after morning milking there was a completely different job to do. The milk was sold retail around Hartland village, much of it was put into bottles, but I also had to fill a four gallon churn, because some people had their jug ready, and milk was dipped out of the churn with a stainless steel one pint measure, and poured straight into the jug. We also filled small, one third of a pint bottles, that were delivered to the village school.

I had filled plenty of milk bottles on my first farm, but now I was required to go on the milk round to deliver the milk. The crates of bottles and the churn were loaded on to a little, flat topped cart, and into that cart was harnessed a pure white pony, called Snowball. She was as fat as a mole, and sweet-tempered too. Her life was a pretty easy one as after the milk round, the rest of the day was spent lazing in the fields, with a few exceptions.

For about a week, my boss went with me, to show me the ropes and introduce me to the customers, then I was on my own. I bought myself a brown drill overall, and unless it was very wet, I wore shoes on the round. I was given a money bag and the accounts book. It soon became clear just how easy going my boss was as some people were owing quite a lot of money, but paying off the debt by dribs and drabs as and when they could. Now the boss's wife was made of sterner stuff, and she told me I must chase up the back sliders, and back it up by threats to stop leaving their daily pinta. It sounded a good principal, but easier said than done. I did try, however, to collect the correct money on Saturdays, to ensure they didn't slip further into the red, and any extra was a bonus.

Having said this, actually this only applied to a very few of the customers, most had their money ready for me on the dot. Even after five years in the big outside world, I was still a bit on the shy side, but that year on the milk round changed all that, and my confidence grew. It was lovely to open people's doors with a cheery 'Milko', and exchange a few words with the customers. The children loved to come over to pat the little pony and she often got odd titbits, apples, sugar lumps and the like.

The very hot summer days posed a problem, nobody had a fridge in those days, and at the farm, water could become short, so that there was none to spare for the ripple-cooler. We bottled up the evening's milk right after milking, and stood the crates of bottles in cold water, a doubtful exercise I guess, because the warm milk would have raised the temperature of the water, so cancelling out any early advantages. And, of course, we began to get complaints about the keeping quality of the milk, and I began to worry about going on the round. My boss dismissed my fears and said the weather was to blame, the hot spell wouldn't last long and it was probably a case of poor storage on the part of the customer. For once in my life, I was happy to see the lovely weather turn cooler.

One funny incident occurred during my time at Ford Farm, when a circus came to Hartland, and in those days, lions and tigers were an essential ingredient of any circus worth the name. When they approached the village, the manager of the outfit went on ahead to find out exactly where they were to set up the Big Top. I cannot remember why, but some problem arose, and whilst this was being sorted out, the circus was advised to pull off the main street and park pro tem on the Bude road, below the Anchor Inn, by Heard's garages. Now this was also the road leading to Ford Farm and it came as a surprise to me, when I was returning from the round, to see all those large vans and lorries parked beside the road. We had seen posters advertising the coming event of course, and had made plans to pay it a visit. Anyway, as I passed by, just holding on to Snowball's reins, I gazed at the various vehicles, with pictures of death defying deeds blazoned across their side.

But then the unexpected happened, one of the caged lions let out a deep-throated roar. To say I was startled is putting it mildly, but the effect it had on poor Snowball was catastrophic. She gave a high pitched whinny of sheer terror — and bolted — the reins being tugged from my grasp in her first mad leap. One could but sympathize as she had never heard a sound like that before, which to her signalled *danger*. She charged up the road, bottles and crates rattling, but miraculously still on board, that is, until she turned sharply into the yard. The nearside wheel met an immovable obstruction in the form of the gate post, the cart tilted to a gravity defying angle, and away went the milk crates, to crash noisily to the ground. But it took more than a handicap such as the said gatepost to halt our Snowball. She plunged on and somehow the cart followed until she came to a halt outside the dairy, there to stand shaking, eyes wild and nostrils flared. By the time I had caught up with her, the boss and workman were on the scene, surveying the damage and trying to calm the terrified animal. My explanation was received with a degree of disbelief, but then I think they realized that it had to be something pretty horrific, and beyond my control, to spook such a gentle creature. We set about picking up the broken glass, and I recall that most of the smallest bottles were smashed, and more than a few of the others. "Ah! well," said the boss, "it could have been worse I suppose, at least they were empty."

CHAPTER TWENTY-TWO

ENTERTAINMENTS

In addition to Snowball, there was a young colt, about two years old of part Arab blood. She was a pretty animal indeed, and it was decided it was about time to 'break her in', in other words, to accustom her gradually to reins, a saddle, and finally a rider, and the local blacksmith was given the task. The colt was halter broken first of all, and spent some time each day, tied up by the halter.

Next came the reins, and this involved getting her to open her mouth to have the bit placed in it. She was led around by the reins and learnt that a pull on the left rein meant that she moved to the left, a pull on the right rein when she was needed to turn that way, and a steady even pull signified stop. The youngsters had made a fuss of her, and she seemed to have no malice, but took the training in her stride, so to speak. We all gathered round and watched when the saddle was first put on her back, and again she raised no objections.

A week later was the big test. The blacksmith got her ready, saddle and all, and after a few gentle words and encouraging pats, swung nimbly into the saddle. If anyone expected to witness scenes from a wild west rodeo, they were disappointed for around the field went horse and rider, first walking, the at a gentle trot, and finally a full gallop. She responded beautifully and we were all full of praise, both for her and the rider, when he stopped and slid off. Looking at the group gathered there he asked, "Who's next?" And so it was, I took the reins and rode her round and round the field. It certainly was no act of bravery, she was just perfect. After that I took her out several evenings a week and we became great friends.

Now as I have already said, Snowball's life was for the most part, a fairly leisurable affair. But at hay harvest, she performed another, harder duty very well, and that more than justified her otherwise lazy days. To help make the hayricks, an elevator was used. It was a far cry from what is in use today, and didn't even look like one. It consisted of a high pole that was made up of sections, and set into the ground beside the rick site. A long beam swung from the top of the pole from which was suspended a large grab. It looked a bit like an oversized spider, with its large spindly legs. It was a clever device activated by a sharp tug on a length of rope. A long rope was threaded through a pulley block at the top of the pole, and attached with big hooks to a draught, or wooden bar, which in turn was attached to the horse's harness. The grab was yanked open and shoved into a pile of hay on the ground beside the rick. Snowball was urged to walk forward, and as she did so, the whole contraption moved upward, the grab closed, thereby carrying to the top of the rick a large amount of hay. Men would be waiting to guide it in over the side and position it over whatever area of the rick they deemed necessary. The leading horse would be halted whilst this was being done, and a clever device activated by a sharp tug on a rope released the legs of the grab and the hay was left on the rick.

Now it was time to make the horse go into reverse, thereby lowering the grab to the ground, where the whole process was repeated. It was a rather monotonous job, to and fro for hours on end, but I kept telling myself it was far easier than having to manhandle it up with a pitchfork. It was certainly a hard few days for Snowball, but she was perfect for the job and responded immediately on demand. I can also recall a few times when she was taken out to the fields with some fencing stakes in the cart, but by and large she had a good life.

Carnivals have been an important part of Hartland life for many years, but in 1948, the carnival was held in November, and was torch lit. The boss's wife and I deliberated long as to what we could do, as it was quite unthinkable that we did not enter. Eventually we decided to use Snowball, and a trap, load it with cabbages, turnips and other produce, and entitle it "Off to Market". I was to be the farmer and drive the pony, whilst my landlady took the part of my wife. We put some ducks into a crate at the back of the trap, and the farmer's wife held a large butter basket filled with eggs and off we went. I think some of the credit must go to Snowball, but between us we won a 1st prize rosette — great fun!

Another source of entertainment was the weekly showing of a film in the Church Hall, where every Wednesday evening, a fair crowd gathered. We felt we were really up-to-date, next best thing to the West End in fact! I think I saw more films during my time at Ford Farm than I had seen before — or since. Everything was geared to getting the work done in time for the show. I believe it stopped for a while in the summer, as people were too busy in the fields or their gardens to have time for such frivolities. I expect the entrance fee was around 1s.6d., add to that a packet of Smiths Crisps for 2d. and it was still a cheap night's entertainment.

I had settled in nicely, enjoyed the work, loved meeting the Hartland folk, and was all set to carry on until such time as Reg and I were lucky in getting a small farm to rent, when suddenly it all came to an abrupt end.

I had been in the habit of going back to Lane Barton from time to time, to exchange news and be entertained to tea. I had casually met the new people who had arrived in the farm across the road, Three Gables, and on one of my visits the Lotts told me that their new neighbours were looking for a Land Girl, and was I interested. In spite of being very happy in Hartland, the thought of coming back to Woolsery was very tempting. For one thing, Reg and I would be closer, he would not have to ride a bike to Hartland on Sunday evenings, and although he now had an ex-Army motor bike, petrol was still strictly rationed. And for another, I suppose I had been so much a part of the farming scene in Woolsery, that I felt sort of homesick for it. I arranged to see Mr and Mrs Uglow, and I think they took to me, and I to them at once, and I decided that I would move back 'home'. I regretfully gave in my notice, packed my kit and found myself almost where I had started nearly six years before.

CHAPTER TWENTY-THREE

CONCLUSION

My new boss was another genial man, easily pleased and considerate. I was very well looked after by the farmer's wife, and two lovely little children completed the family, a girl of around four years and a cute little boy, about one year old. As you can guess, they were a young couple, only about five years older than me.

There were cows, but now it was back to basics, in other words, we had to hand milk there. The cow shed was of the older type, where there were no stalls, the cows being chained up to poles set in front, before the mangers. The chains slid up and down on these poles, so presented no problem when a cow decided to lie down, or get to her feet. My new boss had a keen eye for a bargain, where a dairy cow was concerned, and he had a firm conviction that a cow with only three quarters would produce as much as one with the full four quarters if she was of a true dairy character. And of course, these 'three titters' as they were called never cost as much at market as a cow which was firing on all four cylinders, so he often came home with some bargains.

Most of the cows were quite docile and friendly, but occasionally my boss came home with a misfit. In other words, she could be a bit touchy, and lift her leg, either knocking the milker off the stool, or planting her foot in the bucket. The boss tackled these cows himself, which was most considerate, and I was, as usual, happy in my work.

Now some farmers kept their own bull, but most of them had to take their cows, when the time was right, to a farm the other side of Woolsery, where the farmer owned a large Ruby Red Devon bull. Usually the matter was dealt with there and then, but sometimes the cow had to be left there, until such time as she was fully receptive. The bull's owner was a funny little man and I can remember him scuttling down across his cobbled yard, with a few lumps of cattle cake in a metal scoop with a wooden handle, which he fed to Billy the bull. I could never decide whether this extra ration was to give the bull the strength he would need, or to help him recover after!

But more memorable than that, is the journey we had to take to and from the stud. Imagine one rather excitable cow, taken from her companions in the field, and being driven along to where she couldn't know. Add to that, a few open gates *en route*, a gap in a hedge, or a group of noisy boys in the village street, and the result could be disaster. Actually, we did usually pick out a quiet old cow to take along as well, in an effort to reduce the stress, but that did not always work.

On more than one occasion, I have watched in dismay, as frisky Freda took a hedge like a veteran of Aintree racecourse, and disappeared over the nearest horizon. Now for this whole exercise, a bike was essential. With a bit of luck, one could overtake a speeding cow and be ready to head her past the next gap, leap back on trusty bicycle, and in a rare burst of speed, get in front again. The fact that I had absolutely no brakes that worked on my bike troubled me not at all, but added to the thrill.

I recall on one occasion I completely lost the boss and the two cows. I went through a rough back lane, climbed on top of several hedges and gates, but just couldn't locate them. In the end, I went home, and eventually they all turned up, exhausted, and with a fine old tale to tell.

Looking back, I think it was little short of a miracle that these cows ever became pregnant, although I will admit that the homeward journey was usually far less stressful. To take a cow to the bull, and get her back home again, represented two hours work at least, and of course, there was always the risk that one met another farmer *en route*, with his two cows, and that could be tricky indeed.

Once, my boss asked if he could borrow my bicycle to check on some cattle in a field about three quarters of a mile away. I willingly let him go off on my bike, and thought nothing more of it. However, on his return he reminded me that the bike had no brakes, and when he tried to apply them going down the hill, of course nothing happened. He reproved me sternly for risking my life in this way, and insisted I took the offending machine to the local garage to have it made roadworthy, and he would pay, which I gladly accepted. Actually I thought he looked a bit pale when he came back, can't think why!

Now I guess I would have gone on working at that farm for the foreseeable future, had not fate moved in, and altered everything. For several years, Reg and I had been looking at rented farms and tendering for them. We had had so many disappointments that I was beginning to lose hope.

At first I had been full of expectation, but as one rejection followed another, I had become far less optimistic and so it came as a bolt out of the blue, when we were granted the tenancy of a small holding, just outside Woolsery. This was in early February and we were to move in at Lady Day. My excitement knew no bounds, so much had to be arranged and organized. Because of this, I felt little of the regret I had previously experienced, when I had to tell my kind employers that I was going to leave them. And so it was, that on a glorious spring day, at the end of March 1949, Reg and I were married and moved into our first little home, that seemed like a mansion to me.

For better, for worse, as in all things in life, the die was cast, and what I had at first planned to be a war time occupation only, was set to be my life's work. During the years I had learned such a lot, not only about the land and agriculture, but about people, and I had come to love the area, so much so that I now felt it had become my home. My childhood, and even my school days, seemed to be so long ago, as to be almost unreal, and on occasion I smiled to myself when I thought about how my priorities had changed.

As a teenager, I had three burning ambitions; to be an air-hostess and see the world; to swim the Channel, and to write a book. Well, I did get called to an interview with an airline company, but never went.

Through lack of practice, my swimming prowess rapidly fell back, so that put paid to that. But here I am, writing a book of sorts, so all is not lost!

As I look back over the long years, I realize just how lucky I have been in many ways. To be happy in one's way of life is surely most people's ambition. Of course, in our own business, there were ups and downs, and set-backs that no one could have foreseen. Dappled sunlight in fact.

But to be able to walk across fields that are one's own, to feel that one has a stake, no matter how small, in rich English earth, to be able to lean over a gate and watch a tractor ploughing in a distant field, is surely real living, and symbolizes our inheritance. The land and soil are basics which are real, and to me are beyond price. I sometimes ask myself what would have happened if the war had not come. I believe that to a greater or lesser degree, it shaped the lives of all who lived through it, and I believe it also altered our attitude to life, more so perhaps, for my generation who actually grew up during those bleak years.

There is just one footnote I'd like to add. As the years went by, I became reconciled to my first employer and his wife. They visited us from time to time, and when his wife died and Mr Norris moved into a bungalow in Bideford, I called by on a fairly regular basis. I even managed to visit him in Teignmouth shortly before his death. He had mellowed a lot over the years and who can tell, perhaps I had too! The young can be harshly critical in their judgements, it is either black or white, no room for grey areas.

To the reader I would say that I hope you have been entertained, and even amused, by this story. But most of all I hope that the younger generation who might also read it, will reflect upon the conditions that prevailed only 50 years ago. A very short space of time to see such dramatic advances, not only in machinery but in management and technique. I find it difficult to believe that the next half century can produce such great changes, and even if this does happen, I shan't be around to see it. But I am convinced that whatever happens, there will still be the need for close, hands on contact both with animals and the land.

Without the land we perish, and we misuse it at our peril. But I'm pretty optimistic as I talk with the young farmers I know, and realize the extent of their love and commitment. I am convinced the future of British agriculture is in safe hands, and it will continue to flourish, and feed the nation. Alas! In the crowded cities of our world people are in such close contact that they grind against and shape each other rather like pebbles on a beach, and their feet never touch the land because it is buried under concrete and asphalt.

It took me years to learn that life doesn't come with a plan. To some extent the page is blank, and although you may have a rough idea of where you want to go, you won't get there without making some tough decisions. It is said that if you risk nothing, you risk everything! I think this is truer in agriculture than many other professions.

I'll leave you with a quotation from a book by Henry Brewis regarding the status of older farmers. Before the war they were rejects he says, then became Saviours, but are now an endangered species. For all our sakes, we must slap a preservation order on them.